IMAGES
of America

AROUND WAYNESBORO

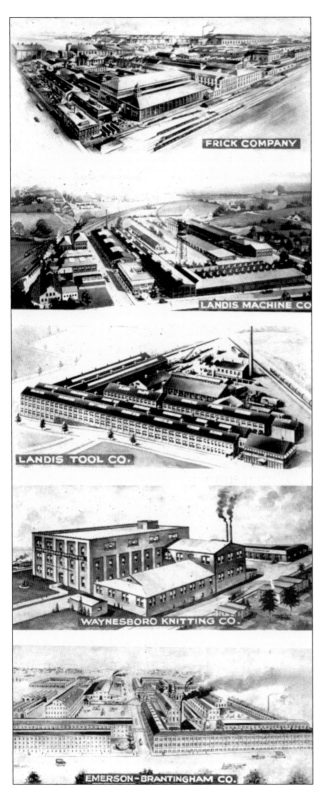

This display panel illustrates five of Waynesboro's major industries during one of the town's most prosperous periods, in the early 1920s. From top to bottom are Frick Company, Landis Machine Company, Landis Tool Company, Waynesboro Knitting Company, and Emerson-Brantingham Company (formerly Geiser). (Courtesy of the Robert Ringer family.)

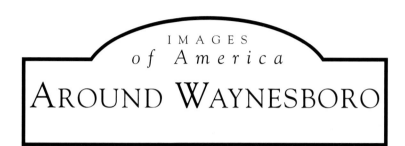

IMAGES
of America

AROUND WAYNESBORO

David W. Thompson with the
Waynesboro Historical Society

ARCADIA

Copyright © 2003 by David W. Thompson with the Waynesboro Historical Society
ISBN 0-7385-3452-8

First published 2003

Published by Arcadia Publishing,
an imprint of Tempus Publishing Inc.
Portsmouth NH, Charleston SC, Chicago,
San Francisco

Printed in Great Britain

Library of Congress Catalog Card Number: 2003110799

For all general information, contact Arcadia Publishing:
Telephone 843-853-2070
Fax 843-853-0044
E-mail sales@arcadiapublishing.com
For customer service and orders:
Toll-free 1-888-313-2665

Visit us on the Internet at www.arcadiapublishing.com

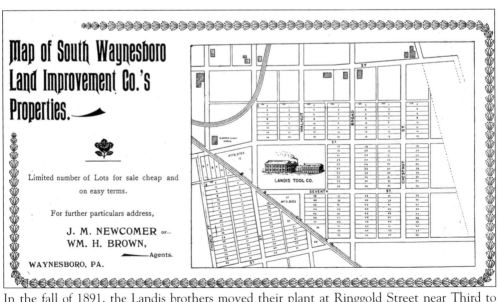

In the fall of 1891, the Landis brothers moved their plant at Ringgold Street near Third to Ringgold and Sixth Streets. The Waynesboro Real Estate Development Company, formed to develop south Waynesboro, offered the company free land to make the move. In the days before the automobile, workers actually wanted to live close to factories. This is an 1897 advertisement for property near Landis. (Courtesy of the Robert Ringer family.)

CONTENTS

ACKNOWLEDGMENTS

Obviously, it would be hard to produce a book of historical photographs if there were no photographs available to put into it. Fortunately, Waynesboro has been blessed with many local residents who have been willing to keep the record.

Many photographs from the Waynesboro Historical Society—which has collections from such well-known local photographers as Daniel Frankforter, Charles Besecker, and others—have been included in this book. Recently, much of the wonderful, voluminous collection amassed by the late local historian Robert L. Ringer has been moved to the society's Oller House headquarters. Bob's daughter, Nancy Frame, and brother, Donald M. Ringer, have been generous with their time in helping to collect photographs for this project.

Sylvester Snyder, a talented local photographer for many years, has let us use many of his artistic shots covering a period of more than 30 years. Mont Alto resident Becky Dietrich, an artist and historian wrapped up in one person, helped us expand the scope of this book with images she has collected of the Mont Alto and Blue Ridge Summit areas and helped with captioning several of the photographs.

Record Herald photographer Sid Miller, one of the most well-known and friendly men in the Waynesboro area, lent some of the pictures he has taken over his long career. Photographs by Dan Arthur, Pat Brezler, and Marie Lanser Beck appear on these pages, as well. It is hard to trace the origin of every old picture, and I am sure there are photographs by others of whom I am not aware. My apologies in advance.

Helpers in preparing text at one time or another have included Elizabeth Rock, Ken Beam, Andrea Struble, James Smith, Ed Miller, Kathryn Oller, and Bill Helfrick and his friends at the Waynesboro Industrial Museum. Special thanks go to William Lawbaugh, who spent several Saturdays helping to research and write.

And I am especially grateful to Brian Sease, who has spent hours preparing the images to be sent to the publisher. Without his help, this book could not have been completed. My wife, Joyce, also deserves credit for her help and for putting up with me over the course of this project.

Many good local histories of Waynesboro are available in the Oller House library. Those written by the late Carl Besore and Robert Ringer, the late W.J. "Wib" Davis, and Jacqueline Barlup have been especially helpful in preparing captions for this project.

This book is a historical record, but I make no claim for completeness. More than 200 photographs are included, but there are hundreds more that could have been included. Unfortunately, choices had to be made. Every attempt has been made to ensure the accuracy of the information in this book. If there are errors, the blame is mine.

My hope is that readers, whether familiar with Waynesboro or not, will enjoy this look at the borough's past.

—David W. Thompson
September 2003

INTRODUCTION

It makes a nice story. Revolutionary War hero and Indian fighter Gen. "Mad Anthony" Wayne, while watering his horse at a stream near the site of present-day Waynesboro, remarked, "What a beautiful place to build a town."

That is the legend. What is known is that Scottish-Irish settler John Wallace laid out the town that was to become Waynesboro in 1797. Wallace was an admirer of General Wayne, having served under him at the Battle of Stony Point, New York.

The area that is now Waynesboro borough was settled in the 1750s. It was previously called Mount Vernon by Wallace's father, an early settler also named John, and was also known as Wallacetown. When first incorporated in 1818, the town was named Waynesburg. But the name was contested by several other towns in Pennsylvania of the same name. When the federal government decided that post offices in one state could not have the same name, the town was reincorporated as Waynesborough, later shortened to Waynesboro in 1831.

The younger Wallace's 1797 plat was described as being "along the country road leading from Greencastle to Baltimore threw [sic] John Wallace's town also called Waynesburg." The town square, still located in the same spot today, also included the north-south road from the Franklin County seat of Chambersburg to Hagerstown, Maryland.

The crossroads location served Waynesboro well. The first turnpike through town was built in 1816 and was a major route between Baltimore and Pittsburgh. Blacksmith shops, wagon makers, and harness shops sprang up to serve the travelers. Nearby furnaces at Mont Alto, Pine Grove, and Caledonia ensured that there were goods to carry along the roads.

Mills ground the grain of area farms. Tanneries, such as Royer's and Forney's, supplied leather for distant markets. Near what is now the southwest corner of South Potomac and Main Streets, local artisan John Bell had a thriving pottery operation. By 1830, Waynesboro had between 140 and 150 dwellings and businesses and a population of 888.

The town's first bank, the Waynesboro Saving Fund Society, was established on March 5, 1853, and was succeeded by the First National Bank on November 18, 1863. The slowly growing town's quiet existence was disrupted when it was twice occupied by Confederate troops for a total of 15 days in 1863. Gen. Jubal Early's forces came up from Smithsburg, Maryland, on June 23, and Early's staff used the town hall on the southeast corner of the square for a headquarters.

Although there were a couple of incidents, the troops were on generally good behavior during the occupation and the later retreat from Gettysburg. Gen. Robert E. Lee is said to have dined at Stephey's Tavern in nearby Rouzerville during the withdrawal and also (although it is subject to dispute) to have watered his horse, Traveler, at the Waynesboro pump in Center Square.

In a crucial development for Waynesboro, George Frick brought his shop to Waynesboro in 1861 to manufacture a grain separator patented by local inventor Peter Geiser. Frick set up in a 50-by-100-foot shop on what is now South Broad Street. Deciding to concentrate on producing steam engines, he later sold the separator business to the firm of Geiser, Price, and

Company in 1867 to raise capital.

Still short of funds and lacking easy access to railroads, Frick was ready to move to Hagerstown in the early 1870s, but a group of 13 local citizens came up with $34,000 in capital in 1873 and formed Frick and Company, saving the industry for Waynesboro. When the railroad finally arrived in Waynesboro in 1879, Frick moved to a new site adjacent to the line at the west end of town.

Waynesboro started to take off during this era. Telephone service arrived in 1883, and electrification occurred in 1893. The population grew from 1,988 in 1880 to 5,396 in 1900 and shot up to 11,000 by 1920.

Further impetus to industrial growth came in 1879, when the Geiser Manufacturing Company, looking for engines to power its machinery, bought the steam engine works of Lancaster County's Landis brothers, Abraham B. and Franklin F. The Landis brothers moved to Waynesboro to work for Geiser, and the ingenious designs they developed there led them to start their own factory manufacturing grinding and boring machines in 1890. Landis Tool came out of that company in 1897, and Landis Machine followed in 1903. It is hard to overestimate the inventive prowess of the Landis brothers. Both are members of the American Precision Museum's Machine Tool Hall of Fame, which has fewer than 50 members.

As Waynesboro's factories grew, more workers were hired and more wealth was created. Downtown Waynesboro had stores of all kinds, and stately homes appeared on borough streets. By 1930, Landis Tool employed 800 workers, Frick 1,200, and Geiser 1,000. Waynesboro's average per capita wealth of $5,600 was almost double the national average of $2,918 in 1930.

On the Blue Ridge Mountains above Waynesboro, vacationers from Baltimore and Washington took in the mountain air at plush resort hotels and cottages. The Western Maryland Railroad's Pen Mar Park brought thousands of visitors to the area and gave the railroad a thriving business. Waynesboro area residents used the Chambersburg, Greencastle, and Waynesboro Street Railway to travel to Pen Mar for summer fun. A railroad park at Mont Alto, north of Waynesboro, also attracted multitudes of visitors.

Waynesboro industries contributed mightily to America's production in both world wars. Frick delivered hundreds of refrigeration units and sawmills, Landis Tool grinders turned out parts for war machines, Geiser produced military wagons during World War I, and Landis Machine shell tappers threaded millions of shells. The Landis companies and Frick continued to prosper after World War II. Geiser went out of business during the Great Depression. At various times, all three were the largest or among the largest in their product lines.

Today, the railroad resorts are gone, victims of the automobile, and Waynesboro's big companies, none of which are locally owned now, hire a fraction of the number of workers they once did. Waynesboro faces many problems typical of American small towns buffeted by foreign manufacturing competition and malls that threaten downtown small businesses.

Yet Waynesboro, with its unique buildings, scenic surroundings, and proud history, remains a pleasant place to live. Recently, more people from outside the town seem to be discovering Waynesboro's charms and moving in to renovate grand old houses. One gets the sense that there is life in the old borough yet.

One
INDUSTRY AND INVENTION

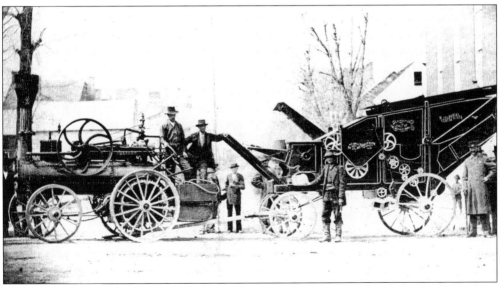

A Frick Company threshing rig is on display in this 1879 photograph. By then, Frick's Eclipse line of steam traction engines was widely known. The Eclipse won the highest award in its class at the 1876 Philadelphia Centennial Exposition. Traction engines pulled plows, ran threshers, and powered sawmills before the onset of gasoline engines. (Courtesy of the Waynesboro Historical Society.)

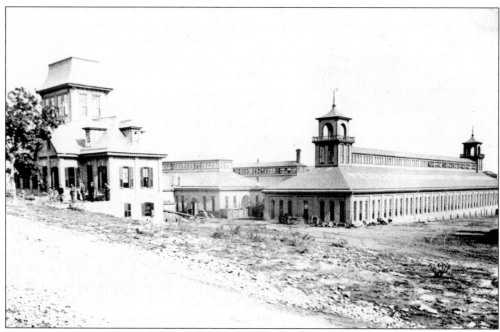

Frick Company, maker of steam traction engines, threshing machines, and other machinery, had outgrown its plant on South Broad Street by the 1880s. The company purchased 12 acres of land from the H.C. Funk farm on the west end of the borough, and the new plant is shown here in 1882 shortly after its construction. The new location near rail lines allowed for easier transportation of Frick products. (Courtesy of the Waynesboro Historical Society.)

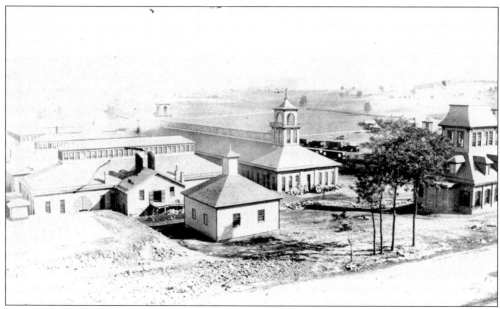

This is how the west side of the new Frick works looked in 1882. Soon after the plant opened, the company established a line of refrigeration products that would become its key to prosperity over the long term. (Courtesy of the Waynesboro Historical Society.)

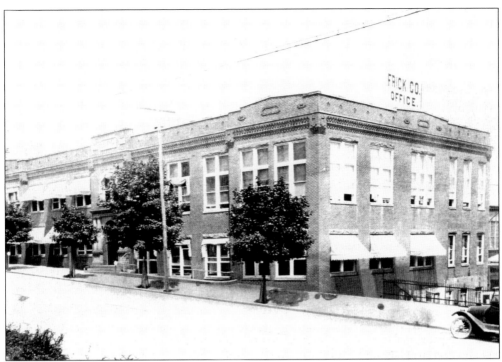

Awnings and trees frame the front of the Frick Company office building on West Main Street on June 6, 1922. Constructed in 1912 and well known to generations of Waynesboro residents, the building was destroyed by fire on November 19, 1988. (Courtesy of the Robert Ringer family.)

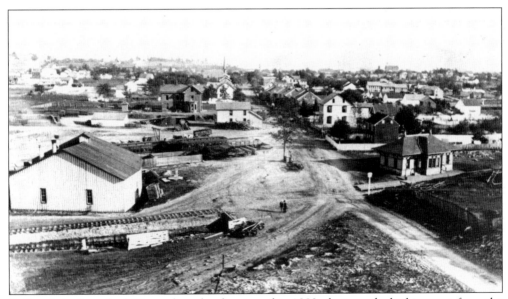

Railroads had reached Waynesboro by the time this 1882 photograph, looking east from the Frick Company works, was taken. Rail transportation was essential for companies like Frick, whose heavy machinery was not easily transported on the roads of the time. The Mont Alto Railroad line had reached Waynesboro in 1879, followed by the Western Maryland in 1881. (Courtesy of the Waynesboro Historical Society.)

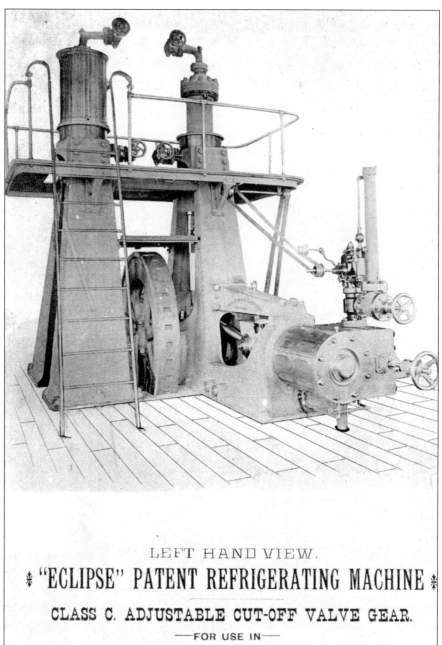

LEFT HAND VIEW.

"ECLIPSE" PATENT REFRIGERATING MACHINE

CLASS C. ADJUSTABLE CUT-OFF VALVE GEAR.

——FOR USE IN——

BEER BREWERIES, PACKING HOUSES, COLD
STORAGE DEPOTS. &C.

(over.)   FRICK COMPANY Engineers, Waynesboro, Pa

Frick Company was established in the refrigeration business by the time this promotional literature was circulating in the 1880s. Abraham O. Frick, son of founder George Frick, made drawings in 1883 for a machine that could develop 25 tons of refrigeration. With the help of engineer Edgar Penney, the company designed large machines powered by Corliss steam engines. (Courtesy of the Robert Ringer family.)

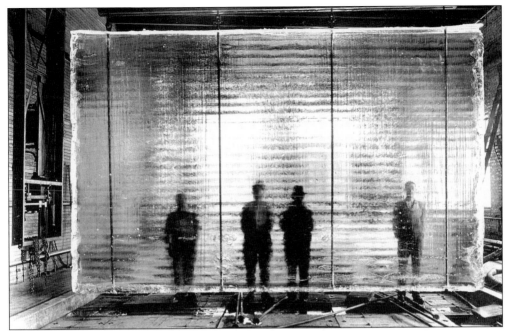

Frick Company employees peer through a sheet of ice made by company equipment in 1885. Using the plate system of production, manufacturers strove to make their ice as clear as possible. The lines in the ice are from chains used to move the sheet after it froze. (Courtesy of the Robert Ringer family.)

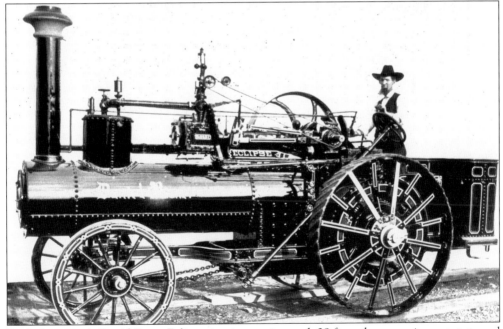

Frick Company's *Daniel Boone* Eclipse traction engine took 39 first-place premiums at state and county fairs in 1885. One observer said the only thing preventing the engine from winning more awards was that "it could only be shown in one place at one time." (Courtesy of the Waynesboro Historical Society.)

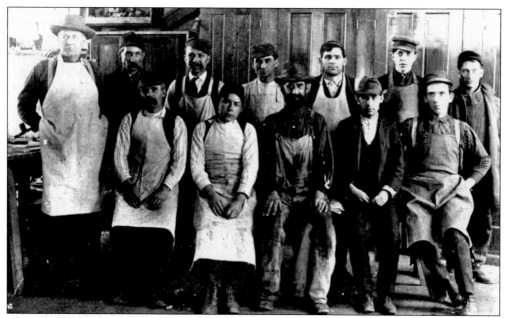

These men comprised the Landis Tool pattern shop force in 1904. Seated, from left to right, are George Byers, Bill Little, Samuel Reynolds, John Motz, and N.B. Zentmyer. Standing, from left to right, are Sam McFerren, Keller Creager, John Little, Ben McNew, Trace Barlup, Frank Hess, and Scott Fisher. (Courtesy of the Waynesboro Historical Society.)

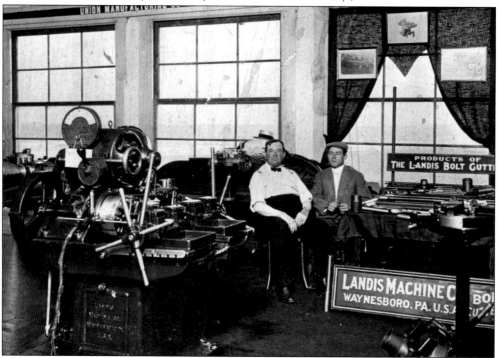

Landis Machine Company workers William Willis (left) and H.W. Marker display products made by the Landis bolt cutter during a machine tool show at the Steel Pier in Atlantic City, New Jersey, c. 1915. (Courtesy of the Waynesboro Historical Society.)

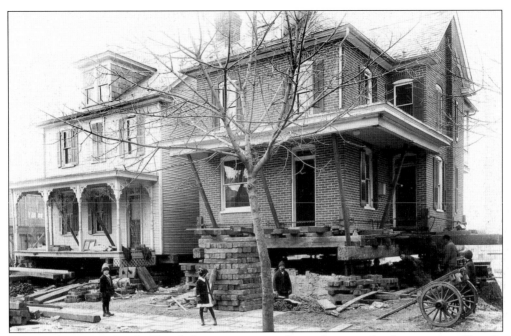

In 1920, houses on South Church Street were moved to make room for the erection of Landis Machine Company's one-story machine shop. Five houses (four brick and one weatherboard) were moved in 1920. In 1928, when the shop was extended, three more brick houses were moved. The work was done by Quigley Hafer of Chambersburg. (Courtesy of the Waynesboro Historical Society.)

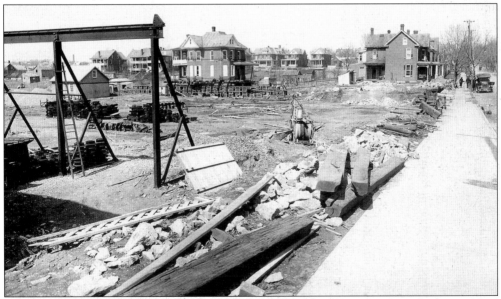

The following houses were moved to make way for the new Landis Machine shop at the time of this 1920 photograph: 328 South Church Street (which moved to 249 South Church), 326 South Church (to 353 South Church), 324 South Church (to 24 West Fourth), 322 South Church (to 40 West Fourth), and 322 South Church (to 34 West Fourth). (Courtesy of the Waynesboro Historical Society.)

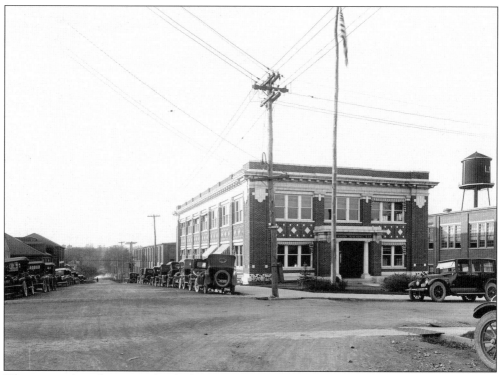

Vintage cars line the streets for the housewarming of the new Landis Machine Company shop on October 30, 1920. The new headquarters building facing South Church Street was a two-story, three-bay structure when built. A third floor and two additional bays were added as the company expanded. (Courtesy of the Waynesboro Historical Society.)

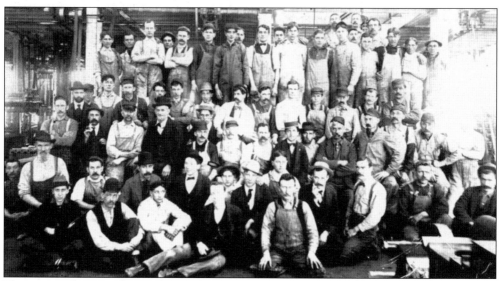

This group of men is the Landis Tool Company workforce of 1902 with the exception of the foundry workers, who for some reason were left out of the photograph. (Courtesy of the Waynesboro Historical Society.)

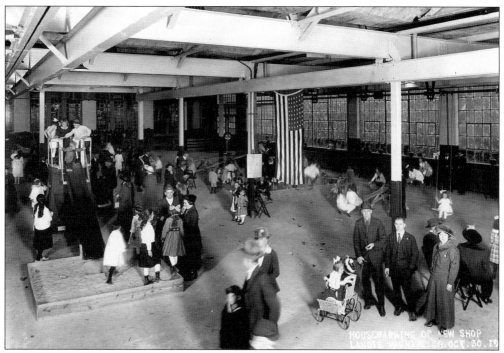

The housewarming for the new shop at Landis Machine Company fell on the day before Halloween in 1920, so plant managers placed pumpkins in the windows and brought in a sliding board, seesaws, and a sandbox to "treat" the children. (Courtesy of the Waynesboro Historical Society.)

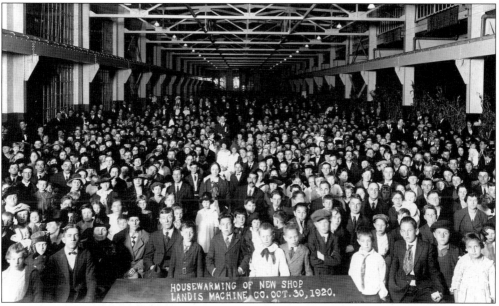

In 1920, Landis was the first machine tool builder to send a sales representative around the world. Closer to home, a new machine shop was built that was a big help in redesigning more capable pipe threading machines. World Wars I and II fueled demand for Landis equipment. By 1964, Landis was the world's largest manufacturer of threading equipment. At its 1981 peak, the company had 775 employees. (Courtesy of the Waynesboro Historical Society.)

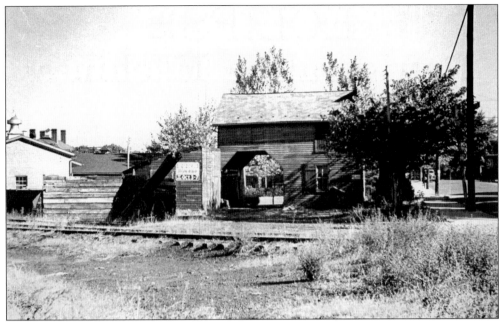

According to photographer and longtime Waynesboro observer Sylvester Snyder, this is the last coal yard in Waynesboro. It was located on South Potomac Street at the railroad tracks near what is now Enterprise Car Rental. By the time this photograph was taken, coal was being supplanted as a heating fuel by oil and gas. (Courtesy of Sylvester Snyder.)

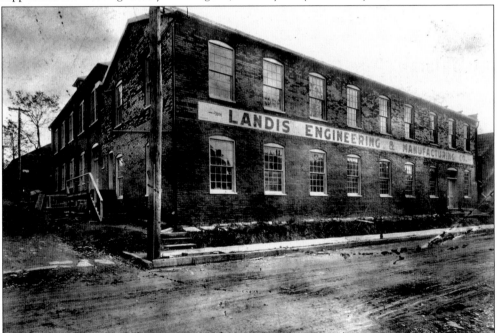

Landis Engineering and Manufacturing Company, at 22 Ringgold Street, was organized by Mark H. Landis, son of F.F. Landis, in 1913 to help continue development of his father's shock diffuser (an early shock absorber). The company also took over the Fred Frick Clock Company, which manufactured electric-time and program-clock systems. (Courtesy of the Robert Ringer family.)

"ECLIPSE"
Refrigerating Machines,

—FOR USE IN—

PACKING HOUSES, BREWERIES, COLD STORAGE DEPOTS, &C.

FULLY WARRANTED

TO BE THE BEST IN THE MARKET, AND COMPLETE IN EVERY DETAIL.

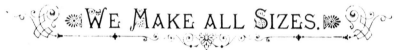

WE MAKE ALL SIZES.

RANGING FROM 1 TO 150 TONS CAPACITY,

And fit up plants complete with Tanks, Boilers, Coils, Piping, Brine Pumps, Special Valves, Separators, Traps, Gauges, and all appurtenances.

We furnish Pure Anhydrous Ammonia for use in our Machines

As this apparatus requires, in nearly all cases, a survey of the premises, in order to give a close estimate of the cost, you will please give full details and a sketch with measurements, and state the kind of work, what amount material is to be cooled, temperatures, or tons of ice, and any information that may be useful in approximating the cost.

Address all communications to

FRICK COMPANY, ENGINEERS,

Waynesboro, Franklin County, Penna., U. S. A.

Due to the Panic of 1884, Frick's refrigeration business started slowly, but four machines of the 1883 design were in use by 1886. The next year, eight more machines were shipped. A giant 150-ton capacity machine was purchased by the Armour and Company meat packing firm in 1887. Famous for their reliability, some early Frick machines were still in use 60 years later. (Courtesy of the Robert Ringer family.)

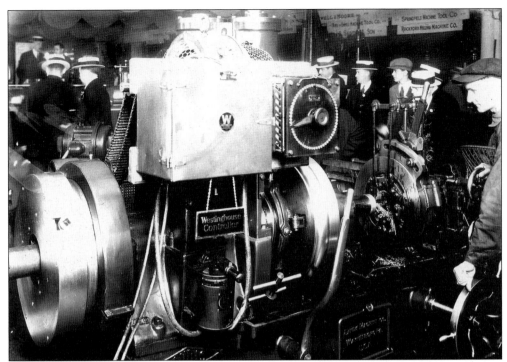

Interested attendees examine a Landis Machine Company four-inch pipe threading and cutting machine at a June 17, 1924, trade show. (Courtesy of the Waynesboro Historical Society.)

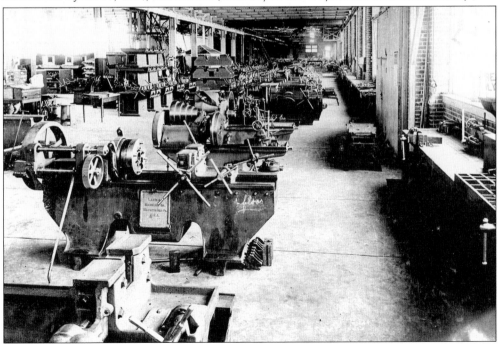

Partially assembled Landis bolt cutters await completion in this view of the Landis Machine Company erecting floor in May 1915. The number of machines under construction indicates that business was good. (Courtesy of the Waynesboro Historical Society.)

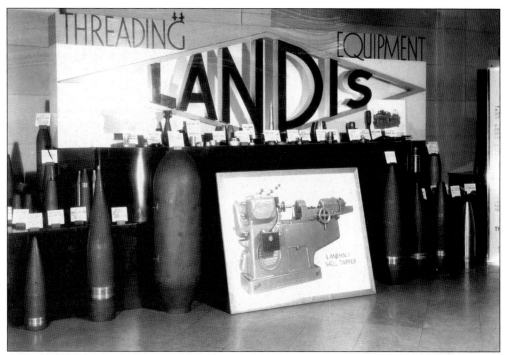

A display at the First National Bank of Waynesboro, on March 21, 1946, shows shells that were threaded on the Landis Machine Company shell tapper. Also displayed are collapsible taps that were applied to other machines. There was enough Landis tapping equipment in operation during World War II to tap threads for fuses in 20 million shells per month. (Courtesy of the Waynesboro Historical Society.)

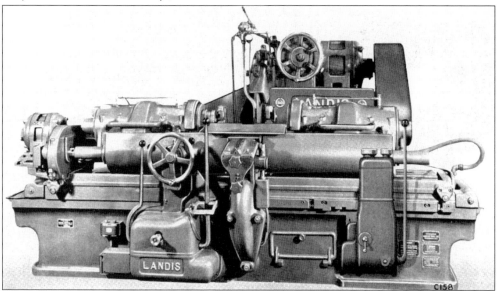

The Landis Tool Company Type D hydraulic crankpin grinder used to produce automotive crankshafts was adapted for use by the aircraft industry in World War II. During the war, Landis worked to improve machines that could grind to more rigid tolerances needed for long-lasting aircraft crankshafts. (Courtesy of the Waynesboro Historical Society.)

21

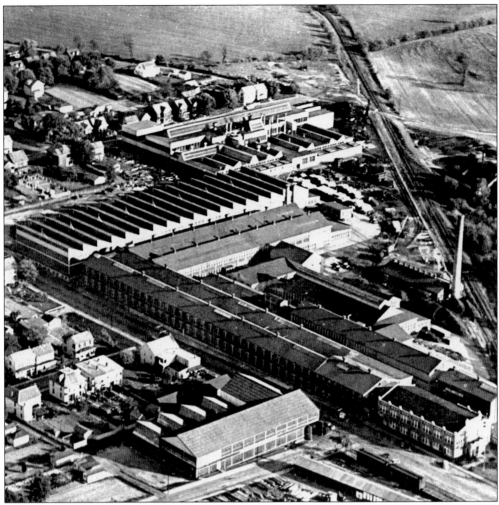

Shown is an aerial view of the Landis Tool Company plant as it appeared on the June 1944 cover of the *Bulletin Board*, published for Landis employees. Employment soared to more than 2,200 during the war, and Landis grinders produced parts for guns, rifles, shells, tools, ships, tanks, trucks, Jeeps, and many other implements of war. (Courtesy of the Waynesboro Industrial Museum.)

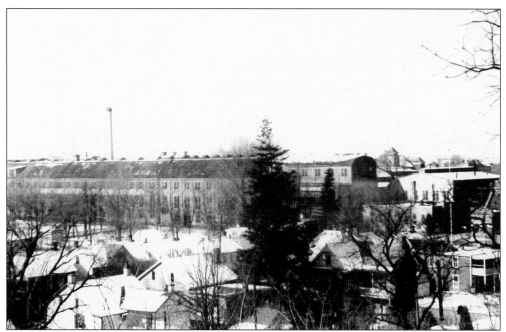

The bulk of the former Geiser Manufacturing Company looms over the relatively new Waynesboro post office (center right) in this 1939 scene. By then, the Great Depression had wiped out local efforts to save Geiser. An August 1940 fire that swept through much of the 13-acre Geiser complex destroyed the Waynesboro manufacturing landmark. (Courtesy of Sylvester Snyder.)

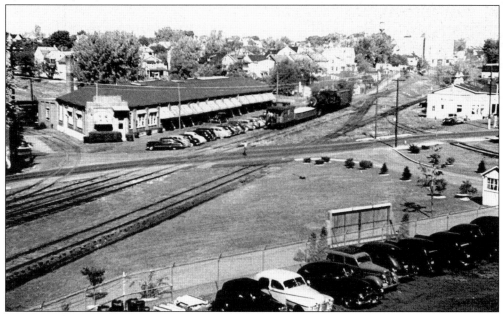

Trains, such as the Western Maryland steamer pushing a load toward South Potomac Street in this 1949 photograph, once serviced Waynesboro's in-town industries. Now these tracks, like others in the borough, are gone, although the right of way can still be seen. (Courtesy of Sylvester Snyder.)

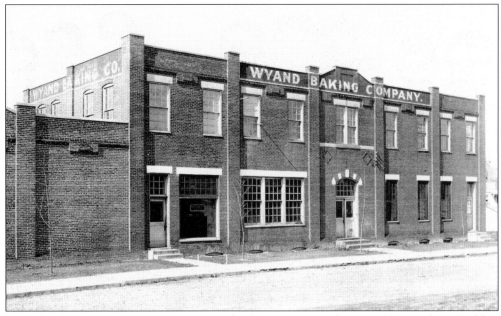

Wyand Baking Company, 130–136 West Third Street, is now the site of Waynesboro Builders Supply. M.L. Wyand, who had previously operated a bakery on Cleveland Avenue, started the business *c.* 1913. At one time, the bakery had a capacity of 10,000 loaves of bread a day, and its trucks delivered into Adams County, Pennsylvania, and Frederick and Washington Counties, Maryland. (Courtesy of the Robert Ringer family.)

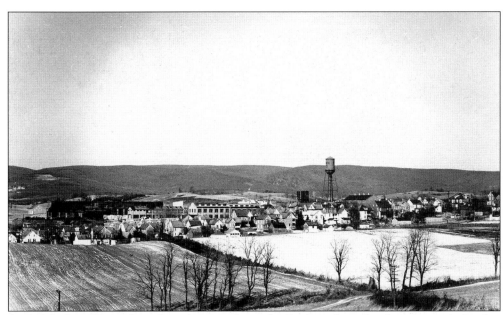

A 1943 look at Waynesboro from the west shows the Frick works under the company's familiar water tower. When Frick moved to the west end in 1881, it opened up development along that side of town. (Courtesy of Sylvester Snyder.)

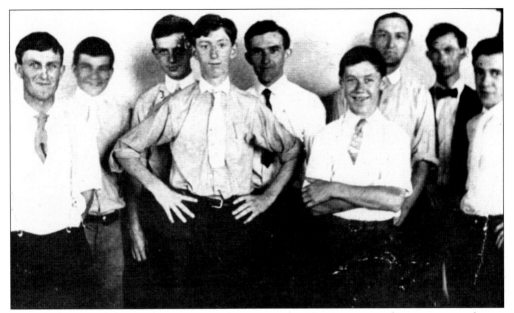

Landis Tool engineer Bert Oller found this picture of 1907 engineering department employees in his attic during World War II. From left to right are Charlie Shockey, Tom Shriver, Don Shriver, Jim Weagley, Harry Beard, Oller, George Lickle, Parker Harrison, and Welty Mathias. (Courtesy of the Waynesboro Historical Society.)

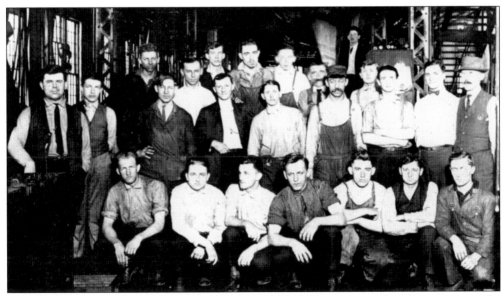

Not all of the men in this 1913 picture of the Landis Tool Company grinding department can be identified, but men with familiar Waynesboro names such as Hess, Fortney, Fitz, Shindledecker, Bowman, and Stoner are among them. (Courtesy of the Waynesboro Historical Society.)

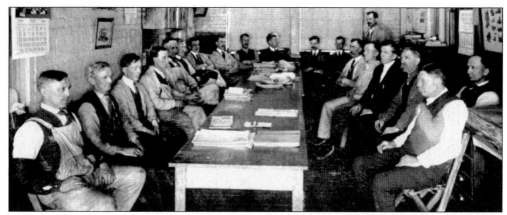

Landis Tool plant foremen assemble in early 1918. Clockwise, from left to right, are Findley Peters, Eddie Shuman, Shorty Fisher, Joe Gorman Sr., Ralph Stoner, Dan Garver, Ed Shriver, Murray Fisher, Howard Paul, H.E. Gray, Les Eberly, Albert Hobbs, Abe Miner (standing), Luther Yingling, Lest McDowell, Jack McDowell, William Strasbaugh, John Neady, and Henry Shank. (Courtesy of the Waynesboro Historical Society.)

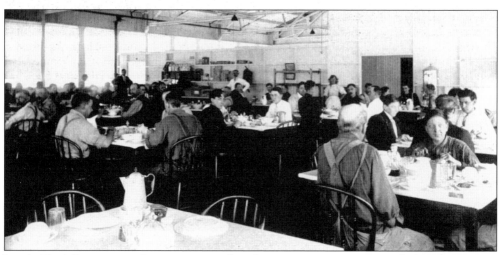

Landis Tool Company workers enjoy a meal in the company restaurant just before the country entered World War I. (Courtesy of the Waynesboro Historical Society.)

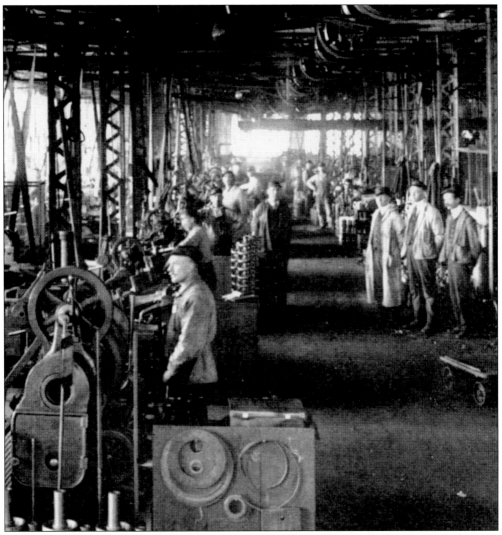

The wife of Landis worker Eddie Hartman snapped this shot of the Landis Tool lathe department during World War I. Landis Tool workers on the western front as well as those in Waynesboro made valuable contributions to the war effort. (Courtesy of the Waynesboro Historical Society.)

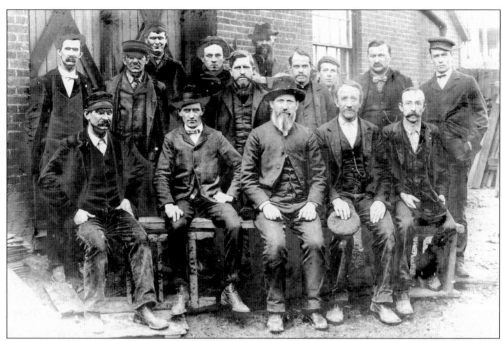

Geiser Manufacturing Company pattern makers take a seat in front of their shop. The man seated in the middle with the hat is John B. Ruthrauff (1853–1910), who was a full-time minister for the Antietam congregation of the Church of the Brethren. He served three congregations: Price's, Welty's, and Waynesboro's. At the time brethren ministers were unpaid, so they had to take other jobs to support their families. (Courtesy of the Waynesboro Historical Society.)

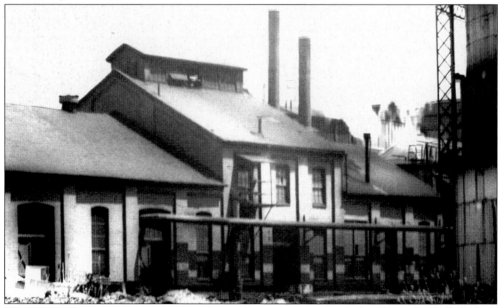

The Waynesboro Gas Company manufactured its own gas at a south Waynesboro plant from train-car loads of coke until natural gas came to town. This is a 1947 photograph of the plant. After natural gas arrived, the Ninth Street facility became a storage area for loads of propane gas. (Courtesy of Sylvester Snyder.)

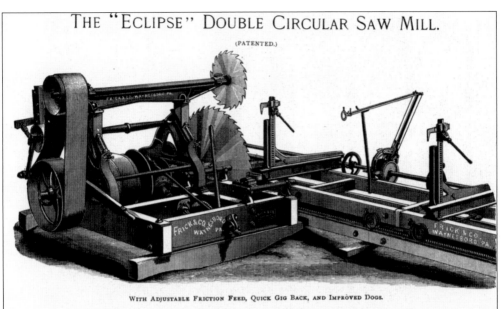

THE "ECLIPSE" DOUBLE CIRCULAR SAW MILL.

(PATENTED.)

WITH ADJUSTABLE FRICTION FEED, QUICK GIG BACK, AND IMPROVED DOGS.

THE above engraving represents our "Eclipse" Double Circular Saw Mill, which we claim combines durability, simplicity, compactness and efficiency with portability. Sawyers and lumbermen will appreciate these advantages.

We invite the most critical examination, while calling attention to some of our points of superiority on pages 58 and 59.

A 19th-century catalog describes the virtues of the formidable-looking Frick double circular sawmill. In days when land had to be cleared and wood was often used as a fuel, portable sawmills that could follow lumbermen and farmers to the job were popular. Frick steam engines often provided the needed power. (Courtesy of the Waynesboro Historical Society.)

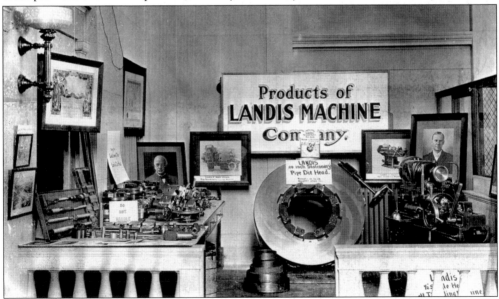

Products of the Landis Machine Company are displayed at the First National Bank of Waynesboro c. 1918. At the back of the display are photographs of Abraham B. Landis, left, and Harry Landis Fisher. Fisher, a member of Lancaster County's inventive Landis family, came to Waynesboro in 1903 and worked his way from designer to superintendent at the Landis plant. He died in 1917 at age 42. (Courtesy of the Waynesboro Historical Society.)

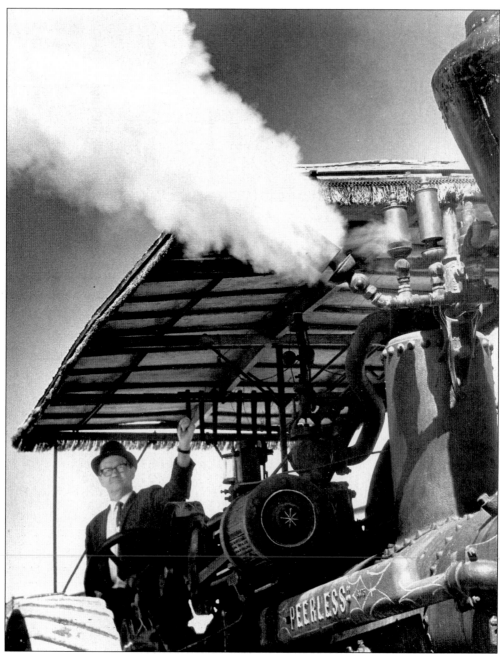

The piercing steam whistle of a Geiser Manufacturing Company Peerless steam traction engine—these days heard at antique tractor exhibitions—was a familiar sound in agricultural regions in the late 19th and early 20th centuries. Geiser purchased the steam engine plant of F.F. and A.B. Landis in 1879 because management wanted engines to power Geiser's threshing machines. (Courtesy of the Waynesboro Historical Society.)

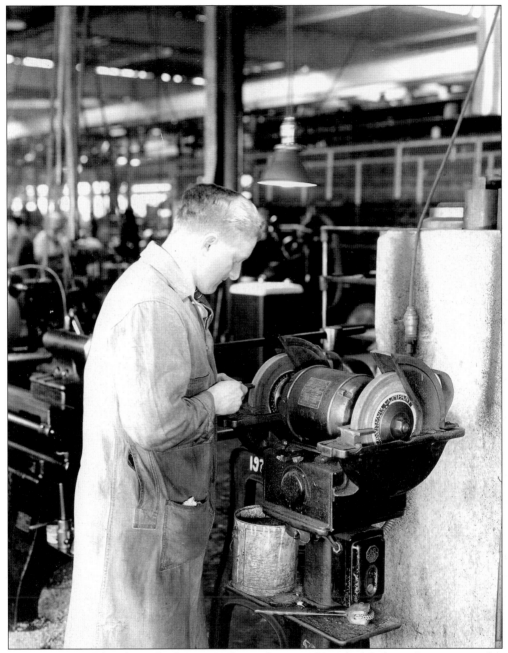

Sidney Benchoff hand grinds chasers in the tool room of Landis Machine Company in this c. 1960s photograph. Products produced by Waynesboro industries had a sterling reputation for quality over the years. Much of that reputation was due to the meticulous work done by men like Benchoff at individual machines. (Courtesy of the Waynesboro Historical Society.)

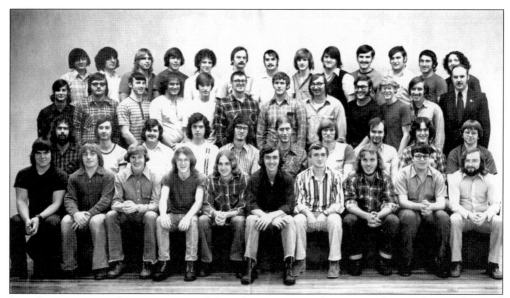

Long hair was in and crewcuts were definitely out among this group of men, the Landis Tool Company apprentice class of 1974. Apprentice classes at Waynesboro industries date back to the 19th century, as some jobs in tool-making industries require extensive training to master. (Courtesy of the Waynesboro Historical Society.)

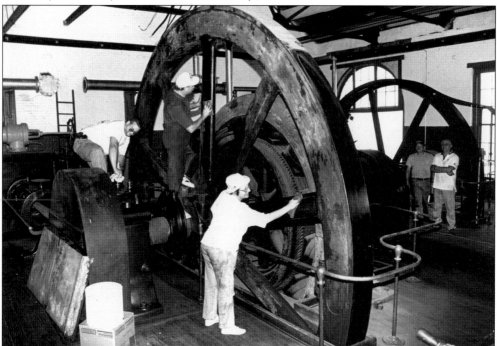

Employees clean the giant 24-ton flywheel of a 1903 Frick cross-compound Corliss engine in the Frick Company power plant in preparation for the 1976 U.S. bicentennial celebration. Although the giant machines that supplied electricity, steam, and compressed air for the Frick plant from 1905 to 1966 are no longer used, they are still housed in the plant on company grounds. (Courtesy of the Robert Ringer family.)

Two
MAIN STREET

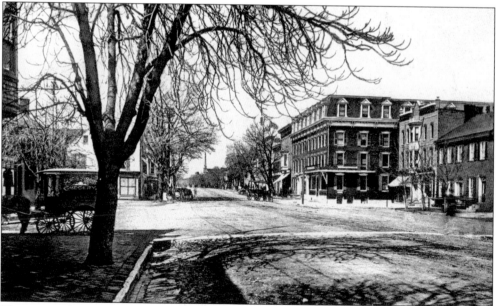

This postcard view depicts Waynesboro's center square *c.* 1910. Prominent on the northwest corner to the right are the Werner Hotel, which had received a fourth story in 1901, the Shively Building, and the Dr. Abraham Strickler residence at the extreme right. The hotel was torn down to make way for the First National Bank building in 1919. (Courtesy of the Robert Ringer family.)

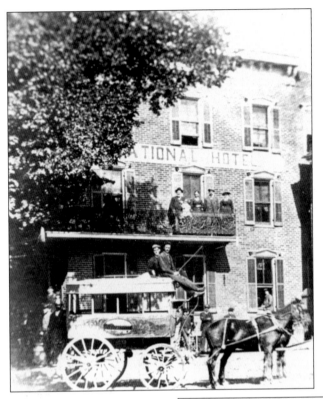

In 1798, Michael Stoner bought a lot in the northwest corner of Center Square from borough founder John Wallace and built a tavern there. By the time this 1882 photograph was taken, the property contained the three-story National Hotel, owned by Jacob J. Miller. The hotel's station wagon used for taking guests to the railroad is parked in front. (Courtesy of the Waynesboro Historical Society.)

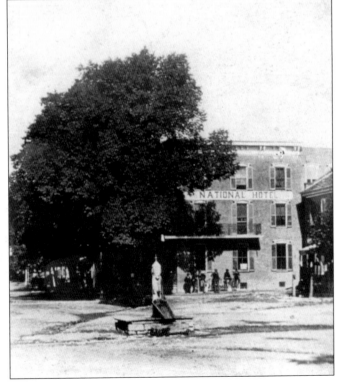

Local legend has a weary Gen. Robert E. Lee, retreating from Gettysburg on July 5, 1863, stopping first at Stephey's Tavern in Rouzerville for a Sunday lunch and then at Waynesboro's town pump (shown in an 1882 photograph) in Center Square for water. The 56-year-old general was cheered as he mounted his horse, rode through town, and headed south down the Leitersburg Pike. (Courtesy of the Waynesboro Historical Society.)

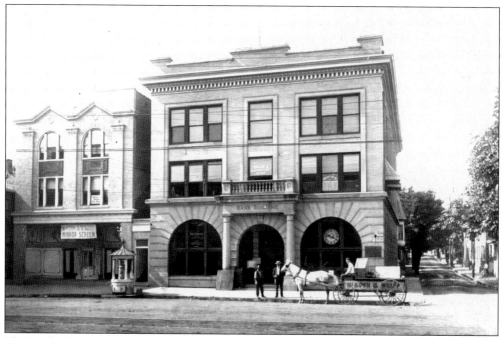

The Bank of Waynesboro, chartered in 1895, rented a room on West Main Street until J.J. Oller sold it a lot at Main and Church on the square for $12,000. The bank was built in 1904 with Oller as president. This photograph of the bank (with the Collins Building housing the Star Theater next door) was taken between 1911 and 1917. (Courtesy of the Robert Ringer family.)

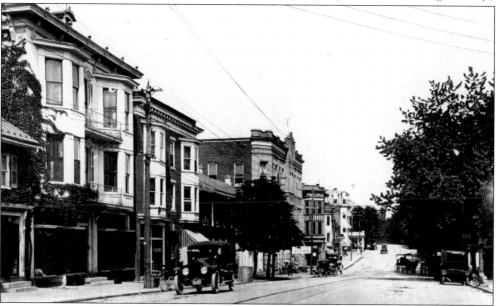

Horses have given way to automobiles and the Chambersburg, Greencastle, and Waynesboro Street Railway track is visible in this c. 1920s view looking west along West Main Street. The large building in the center is the original Wayne Building. Built in 1899, it was destroyed by a January 1930 fire and was replaced by a new, Art Deco–style Wayne Building. (Courtesy of the Robert Ringer family.)

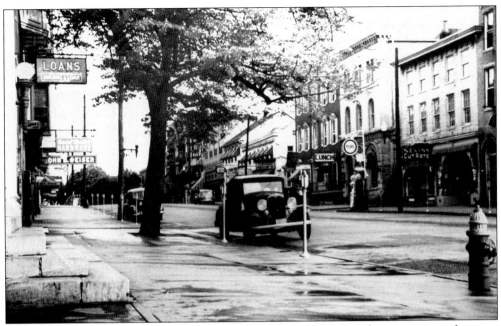

Signs of the Times is the name photographer Sylvester Snyder gave to this streetscape of a quiet, rain-soaked West Main Street in 1938. Note the Pure gasoline pumps located right at curbside—a common practice in the early days of motoring—in front of Nevins Cut Rate store. (Courtesy of Sylvester Snyder.)

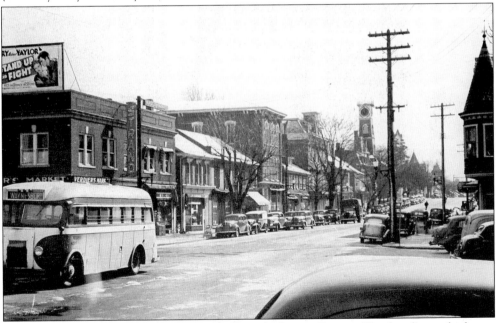

A Gearhart Bus Company vehicle travels through Center Square. The bus line, which was operated by Grant Gearhart, provided service to local communities. Gearhart also operated a service that took workers from the town's manufacturing plants home for lunch and then returned them to the plant. The movie billboard (upper left) dates this photograph at 1938. (Courtesy of Sylvester Snyder.)

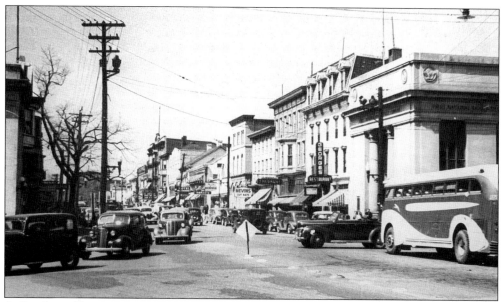

A Greyhound bus stops in Center Square as downtown Waynesboro bustles in this 1941 scene. At one time, interstate and intercity buses were a principal means of transportation for Waynesboro residents. Bus terminal manager Carl Lehman reported that 156 buses came through Waynesboro in a 75-hour period during the 1948 Fourth of July holiday. (Courtesy of Sylvester Snyder.)

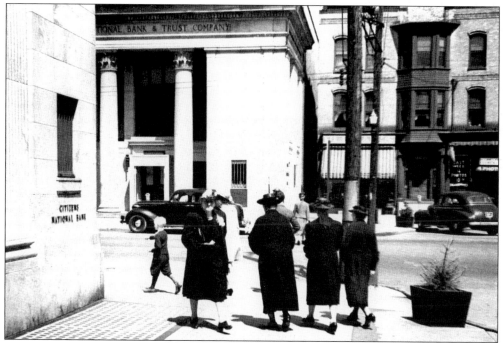

Women wore hats and young boys still wore knickers in Center Square in 1941. Gone, along with the old fashions, is the Shively Building, seen to the right of the First National Bank and Trust. The bank acquired the 100-year-old commercial building in 1961 and had it razed in 1967 to provide expansion space. (Courtesy of Sylvester Snyder.)

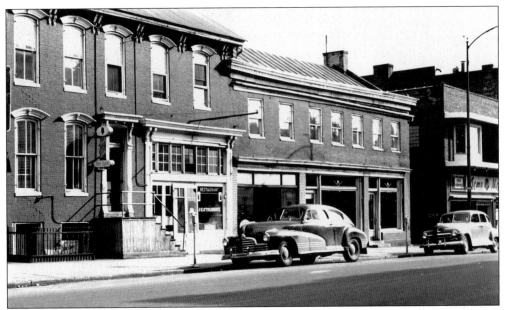

The former Washington Hotel Building, 51–53 ½ West Main Street, was razed in 1953 to make way for a McCrory's store (now Dollar General). The first structure on the site was built in 1819, and many businesses and hotel operations occupied the structure over the years. The downtown Acme Market to the right moved to a South Broad Street building (now occupied by a CVS pharmacy) in 1954. (Courtesy of the Robert Ringer family.)

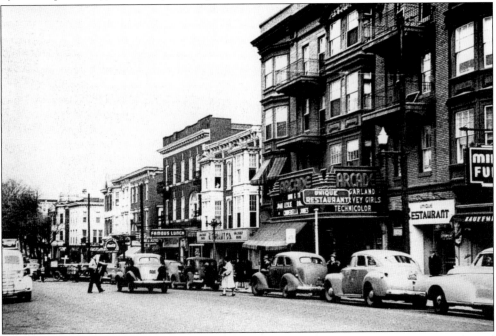

Downtown Waynesboro is a busy place in this 1946 street scene. *The Harvey Girls* and *Cinderella Jones* are the features at the Arcade theater. Businesses such as the Arcade, Famous Lunch, W.T. Grant, Unique Restaurant, and Miller's Furniture have vanished along with the old cars seen in this photograph. (Courtesy of Sylvester Snyder.)

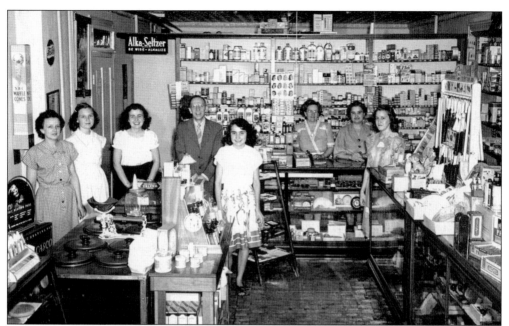

The Economy Cut Rate store was located at 220 West Main Street. From left to right in this July 7, 1947, photograph are the following: Grace Fisher, Frances Diffenbaucher, Margaret L. Coffman, George B. Coffman, Barbara Coffman, Marie Small, Margaret (Mrs. George) Coffman, and Phyllis Coffman. George Coffman was the author of some well-loved local history books. (Courtesy of the Waynesboro Historical Society.)

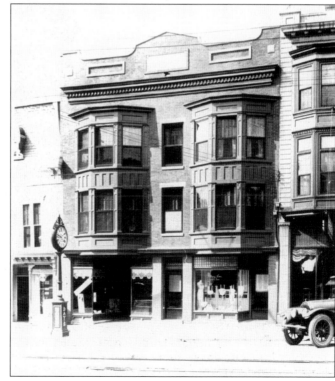

This 1922 photograph of the W.F. Day Building at 26–30 West Main Street was taken not long after the fire-damaged building had been refurbished. William F. Day purchased the building on November 5, 1921, for a price of $22,500. Long Jewelers occupies the building today. The street clock in front of the building was knocked down by a truck in 1937. (Courtesy of the Robert Ringer family.)

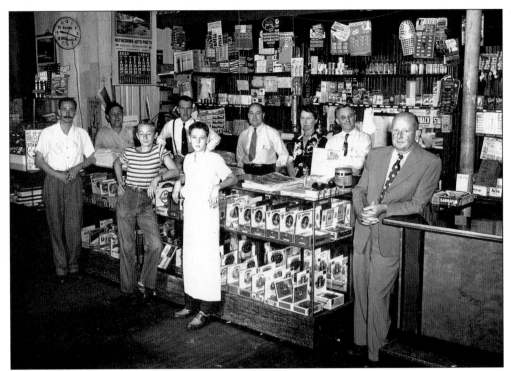

The Waynesboro News Agency on West Main Street was Waynesboro's convenience store before that term was coined. At one time, the agency contained a barber shop and bowling alley in addition to all types of consumer items. From left to right in this 1947 view are J. Wilson "Willie" Heefner, John Jones, Mickey Heefner, Charlie Bumbaugh, Elwood Smith, John H. Funk, Mary Gift, Elmer Smith, and owner R.N. "Bob" Boerner. (Courtesy of the Waynesboro Historical Society.)

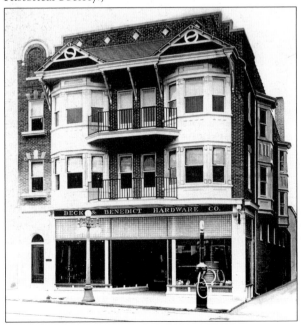

J. Edward Beck and Daniel G. Benedict moved their hardware store from the old Wayne Building into this still-existing West Main Street building in 1916. Beck and Benedict supplied all the dynamite for Pennsylvania Turnpike construction in 1938 and 1939, including the Blue Mountain and Sideling Hill tunnels. Their sons ran the store (shown in this *c.* 1920s photograph) until 1955. (Courtesy of the Waynesboro Historical Society.)

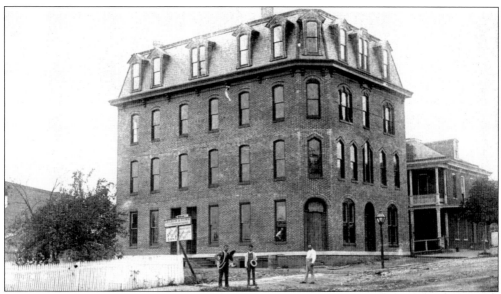

This is the Leland Hotel shortly after it was built in 1888 by Oscar Good. Good had operated a distillery on Red Run near the Waynesboro-Monterey Turnpike before coming to Waynesboro. Although the hotel did well, Good's creditors put it up for sheriff's sale, and Daniel Barnett bought it for $8,000 in 1889. Barnett owned the building until 1916. (Courtesy of Becky Dietrich.)

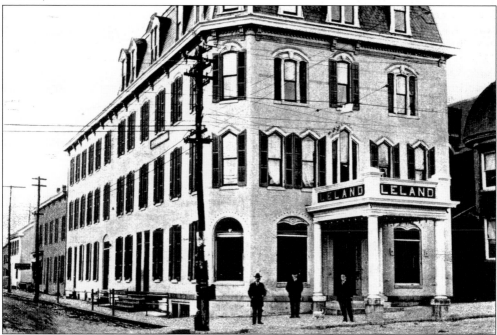

A 1907 view of the Leland Hotel shows additions that had been made since the building was constructed in 1888. Inside, it had a large gentlemen's club room and a dining room. The Leland was renamed the Anthony Wayne for much of the 20th century. The grand old building on West Main Street has survived several fires and is now an assisted-living facility. (Courtesy of the Robert Ringer family.)

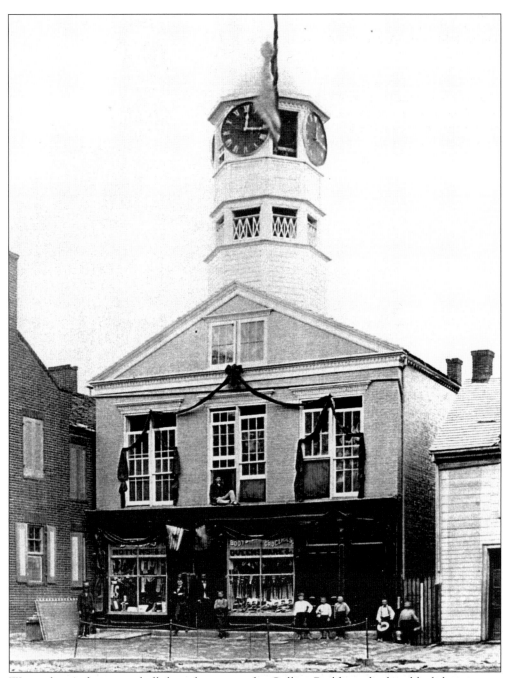

Waynesboro's first town hall, later known as the Collins Building, displays black bunting on April 15, 1865, in memory of Pres. Abraham Lincoln's death. Built in 1853, the building—extensively altered and minus the cupola—still stands on the southeast corner of Center Square. Newspapers, movie theaters, and the Ullman and Painter law offices have been among its occupants. (Courtesy of the Robert Ringer family.)

Borough hall on East Main Street was built in 1881 as the Academy of Music and hosted band concerts, recitals, graduations, lectures, and vaudeville acts. In 1906, the first motion picture in Waynesboro was shown here. When this 1910 photograph was taken, the building was hosting *The Yankee Doodle Boy*. (Courtesy of the Borough of Waynesboro.)

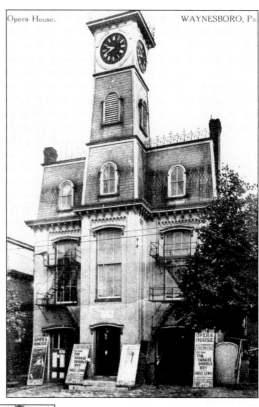

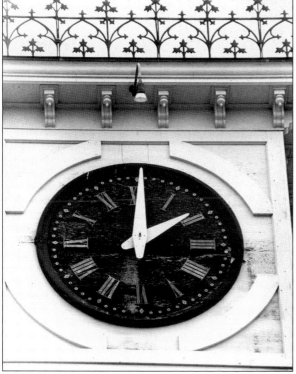

Waynesboro's town clock was installed in 1850 and moved from the old town hall to its present location in 1880. The time mechanism, electrified in 1960, was originally powered by heavy weights on a cable. The clock's bell, forged in Philadelphia in 1850, is the original and would have tolled for Civil War troops marching through town. (Courtesy of Sid Miller, the *Record Herald*.)

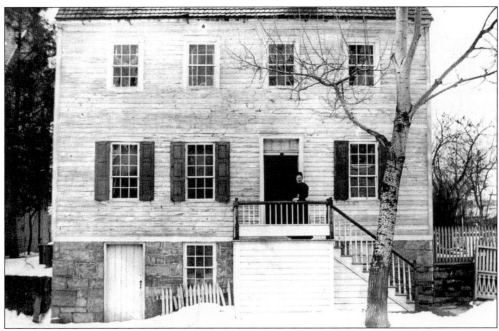

The cabinet shop of Gen. James Bourns, located at 67 East Main Street, was an early Waynesboro landmark. Bourns, a War of 1812 veteran, moved into a house next door in 1816, purchased the lot to the east, and built this structure. The house was purchased by the Joe Stickell American Legion Post No. 15 in 1947 and demolished in 1950 to make room for a legion addition. (Courtesy of the Waynesboro Historical Society.)

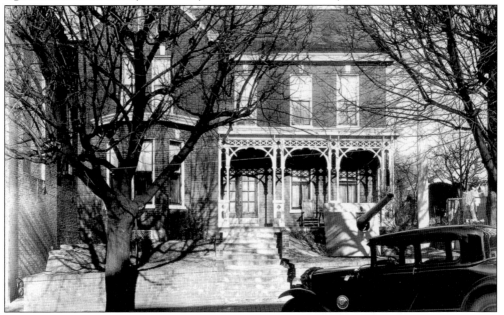

Once the home of W.S. Amberson Sr. and family, this stately brick house at 65 East Main Street was built in 1881. The house was bought by the Joe Stickell American Legion Post No. 15 in 1933, the year this photograph was taken. The war surplus cannon in front of the post was cut up for a scrap drive during World War II. (Courtesy of the Waynesboro Historical Society.)

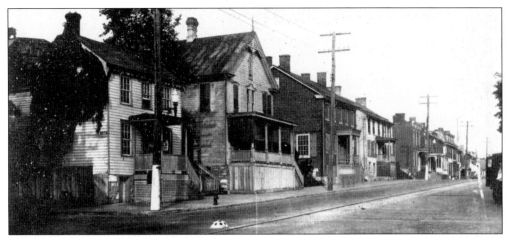

When the Emerson-Brantingham Company sold out in 1925, homes built by the Geiser Manufacturing Company in the late 1800s as employee rental housing were put up for sale. Eight of the dwellings shown in the foreground of this photograph were demolished in the 1930s to make way for the new Waynesboro post office at East Main and South Broad Streets. (Courtesy of the Waynesboro Historical Society.)

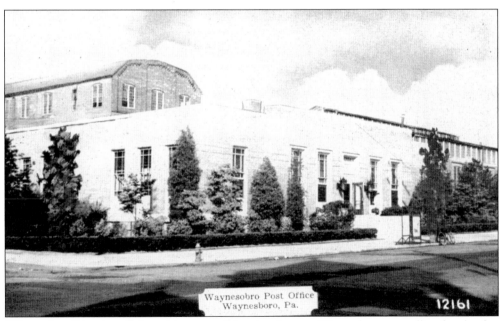

"Waynesboro" is misspelled on this postcard showing the new Waynesboro post office shortly after its completion in 1936. Eight houses built as employee rentals by the Geiser Manufacturing Company were demolished to make way for the post office. The old Geiser works, which can be seen behind the post office, were destroyed by fire in 1940. (Courtesy of the Robert Ringer family.)

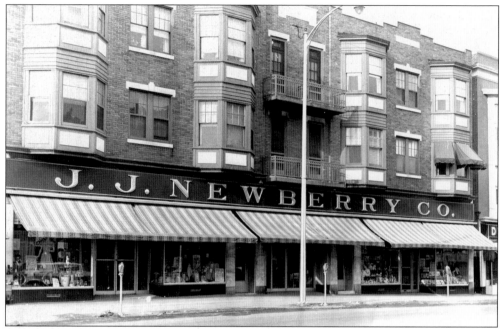

Waynesboro, like most towns, had its share of 5- and 10-cent stores, but all have fallen victim to giant discounters and shopping malls. The J.J. Newberry store at 58–68 West Main Street was located in the new Kirson Building, which was erected after a 1924 fire in the old Kirson Block. Newberry eventually sold the building to Elks Lodge No. 731, the building's present owner. (Courtesy of Brian Sease.)

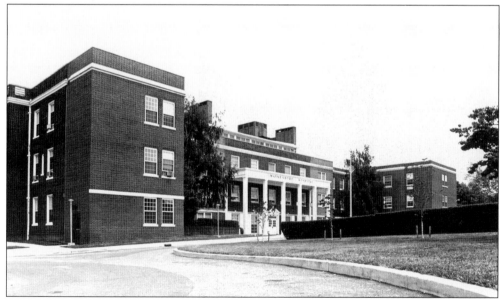

The horrific flu epidemic of 1918 killed 40 Waynesboro residents in a two-week period and convinced the townspeople that a hospital was needed. A pledge drive in 1920 obtained $327,000 from 3,122 subscribers, and a new hospital opened October 2, 1922. This is a 1970s view of the hospital before a three-story addition greatly expanded the emergency room and other facilities. (Courtesy of Sid Miller, the *Record Herald.*)

While downtown Christmas decorations in Waynesboro are not as elaborate as in former times, the borough still sets up a large evergreen tree each year in Center Square. High winds and errant motorists have tilted or toppled the tree at times, but the tradition continues. (Courtesy of Sid Miller, the *Record Herald*.)

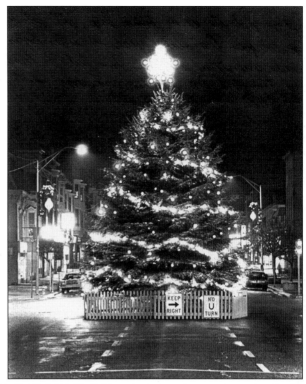

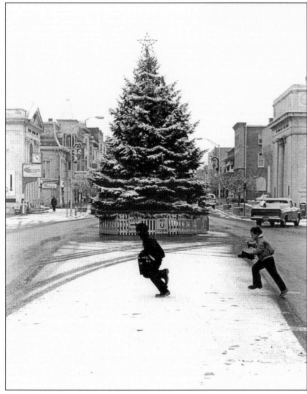

This view shows snowy sidewalks, Waynesboro's traditional tree on Center Square, and kids dashing across Main Street, their minds already on the approaching Christmas break from school. (Courtesy of Sid Miller, the *Record Herald*.)

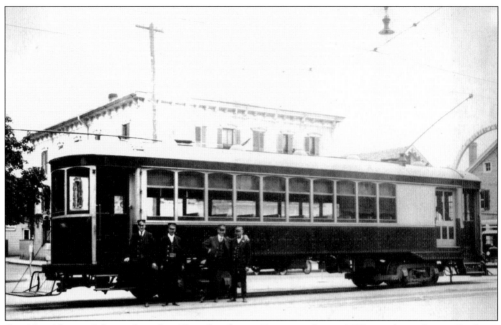

Car No. 35 was delivered to the Chambersburg, Greencastle, and Waynesboro Street Railway in 1920. The railway, which began operations in 1903, was at its peak at the time, running to Pen Mar Park, Greencastle, Chambersburg, and points beyond. The line carried 865,000 passengers in 1924, but the automobile won out, and operations ceased in 1932. (Courtesy of the Robert Ringer family.)

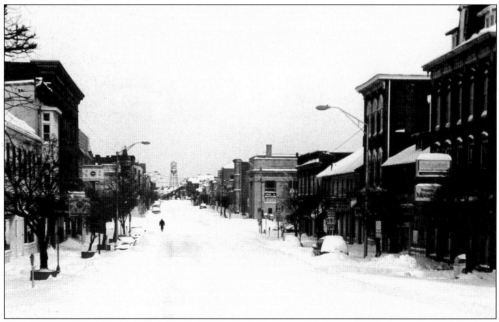

Waynesboro is not known for unduly harsh winters, but occasionally Mother Nature does spring a surprise on the borough, as shown in this barren Main Street scene during the blizzard of 1993. Pennsylvania's mountainous terrain usually breaks up storms approaching from the west, but those sweeping up the valley from the south are another matter. (Courtesy of Patrick Brezler.)

Three
ARCHITECTURAL GEMS

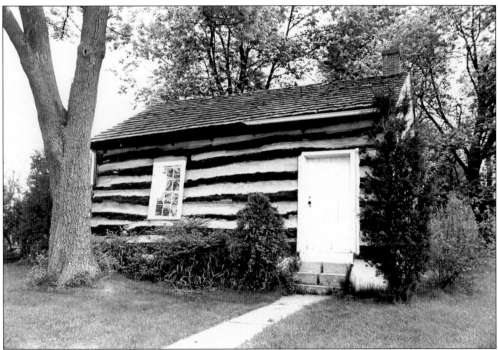

The John Bourns Meetinghouse (c. 1770–1780), located just east of Burns Hill Cemetery, served as the first school-church structure in Waynesboro until churches and schools were built in the early 1800s. Blacksmith and sickle-maker John Bourns came to Roadside, 3 miles north of Waynesboro, c. 1774. He was possibly one of the meetinghouse builders, or the maker of its hardware. (Courtesy of the Waynesboro Historical Society.)

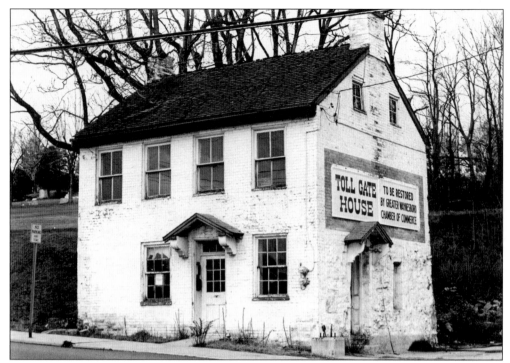

Rundown and abandoned, the Toll Gate House on East Main Street was bought in 1969 for $6,000 by Roy S.F. Angle, who donated it to the Waynesboro Beneficial Association as a headquarters for the Greater Waynesboro Chamber of Commerce. Robert W. Brown, owner of Waynesboro Construction Company, did a $17,000 restoration job at cost. (Courtesy of Brian Sease.)

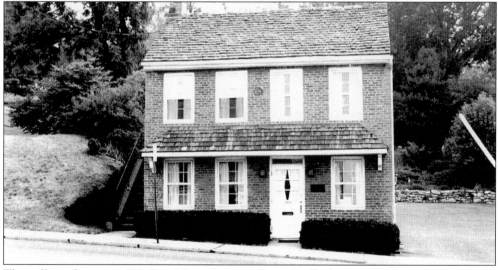

The tollgate house at 323 East Main Street collected tolls from c. 1846 until after World War I. The Waynesboro, Greencastle, Mercersburg Turnpike Company bought the site in 1828 for $80. After World War I, the tollhouse was used as a tavern, grocery store, filling station, and used-car lot before it was donated to the chamber of commerce. (Courtesy of the Waynesboro Historical Society.)

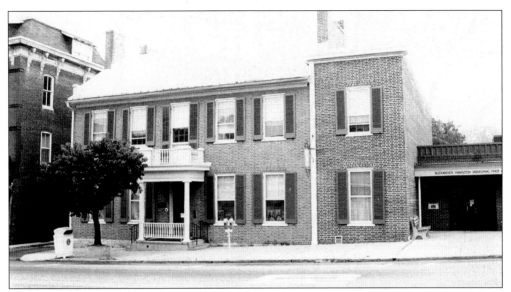

The Alexander Hamilton House at 45 East Main Street, now the Alexander Hamilton Free Library, is a Federal-period structure that was built in 1814. Alexander Hamilton, one of Waynesboro's first real-estate developers, added the porch when he bought the house in 1841. The house became a library in 1955, when Hamilton descendant Jane Yost willed it to the borough. It was modernized in 1978, and a wing was added in the late 1980s. (Courtesy of the Waynesboro Historical Society.)

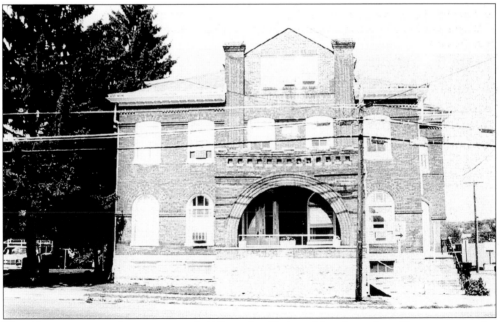

The Romanesque administration building for Geiser Manufacturing Company on the northwest corner of Walnut and East Second Streets was built in 1890. Office workers handled payroll for 175 plant workers and business in excess of $200,000 a year when it opened. Now an apartment building, the structure is the lone survivor of the once-huge Geiser complex. (Courtesy of the Waynesboro Historical Society.)

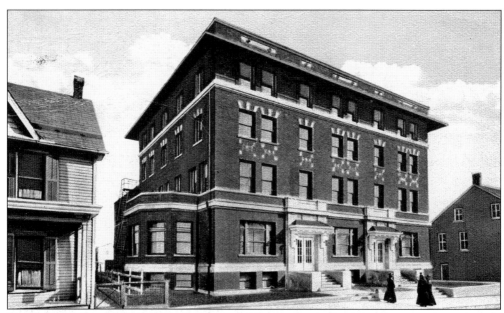

Waynesboro's first YMCA on North Potomac Street was given birth by the evangelistic crusade of Dr. William E. Biederwolf, who came to town in 1914. Biederwolf urged that a YMCA be founded in Waynesboro. Men responded favorably, and the board of trade almost immediately pledged $25,000. The building was dedicated on November 17, 1915. It was torn down years ago, and the Trinity House building now stands on the site. (Courtesy of the Robert Ringer family.)

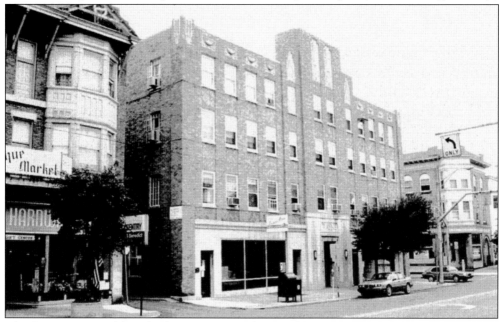

The first Wayne Building, built in 1899, was destroyed by fire in 1929. A year later, an Art Deco Wayne building went up on the same site at 90–94 West Main Street. The top floors have been used as residential apartments, while the bottom two floors have been leased to the telephone company, a drugstore, clothing stores, barber and beauty shops, lawyers, doctors, and others over the years. (Courtesy of the Waynesboro Historical Society.)

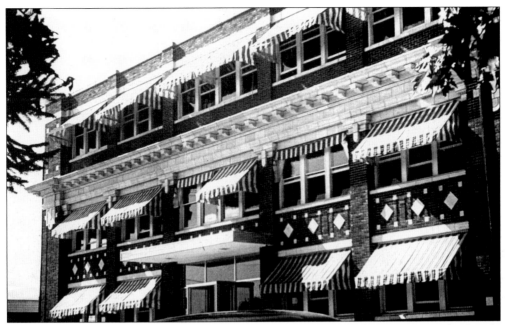

Once a common sight during warm weather, awnings, such as these covering the Landis Machine Company office building windows in 1949, are seldom seen today. The Landis building, erected in 1920, is the borough's lone example of Sullivanesque architecture with its geometric ornamentation and stylized details. (Courtesy of Sylvester Snyder.)

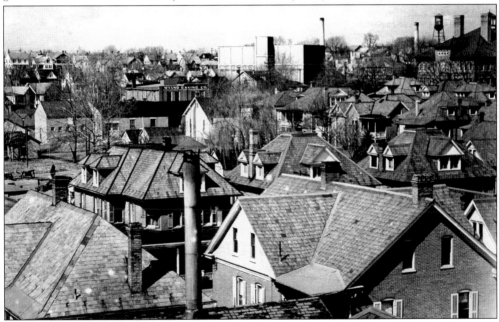

Visible over the rooftops in this 1946 view of Waynesboro are Wyand Baking Company, Waynesboro Ice and Cold Storage Company, and the Snider Avenue School. The ice and cold storage company, which ceased operations a few years ago, once stored apples from area orchards and made ice in blocks as heavy as 300 pounds. Snider Avenue School, built in 1902, is now a luxury apartment building. (Courtesy of Sylvester Snyder.)

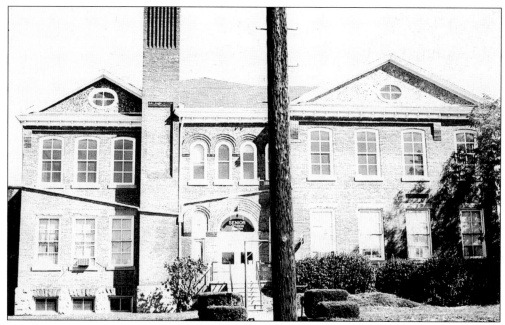

A full acre of land for the North Street School sold for $1,700 in 1891, and it cost only about 10 times that much for A.M. Good and Brothers, a local firm, to build the school. In 1976, the building was leased as the Waynesboro Senior Citizen Center. Abandoned in the mid-1990s, its condition is deteriorating. (Courtesy of the Waynesboro Historical Society.)

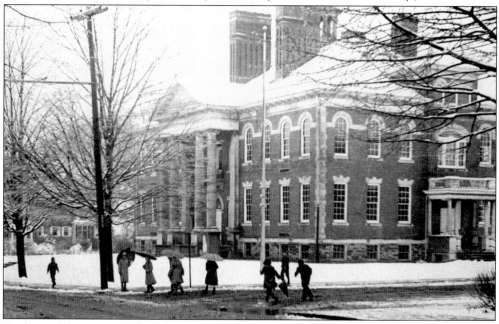

Students did not generally ride buses in the old days, so some of the tales parents and grandparents tell about hiking to school may be true (if sometimes exaggerated). Here, students and adults brave a 1953 storm to reach the grand old Clayton Avenue School, once the borough's high school and now headquarters for the Waynesboro Area School District. (Courtesy of Sylvester Snyder.)

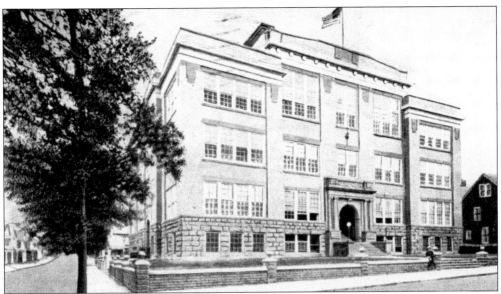

The Waynesboro High School, at the intersection of South Potomac Street and Snider Avenue, was considered the borough's first modern high school when it opened in 1912. It boasted 19 classrooms, 2 science laboratories, a gymnasium, an auditorium, and a shop. When a new high school opened in 1937, the building became a junior high and later West Junior High. The building was demolished in the early 1970s and is now a church parking lot. (Courtesy of the Robert Ringer family.)

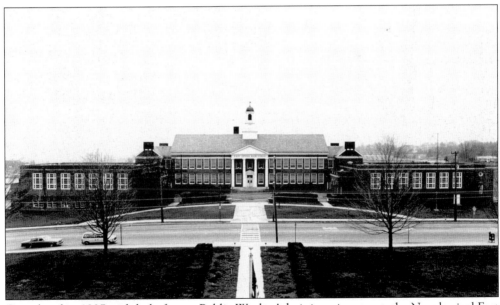

Completed in 1937 with help from a Public Works Administration grant, the Neoclassical East Junior High School building, at 550 East Main Street, served as Waynesboro's high school until 1962. After it was abandoned during a district-wide consolidation in 1989, Waynesboro Hospital purchased it in 1990 for $570,000. The building was demolished in 1999 by the hospital and its corporate owner, Summit Health. (Courtesy of Sid Miller, the *Record Herald*.)

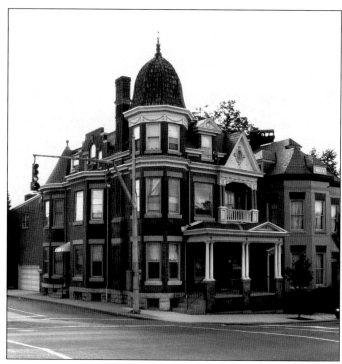

Sollenberger House at West Main and Grant Streets was built before the turn of the 20th century for Willis W. Franz, a manufacturer turned journalist. M.E. Sollenberger, a retired banker and principal of the high school on Clayton Avenue, bought it in 1901. The Queen Anne–style house is dominated by a round tower with a copper-shingled dome and elaborate finial. (Courtesy of the Waynesboro Historical Society.)

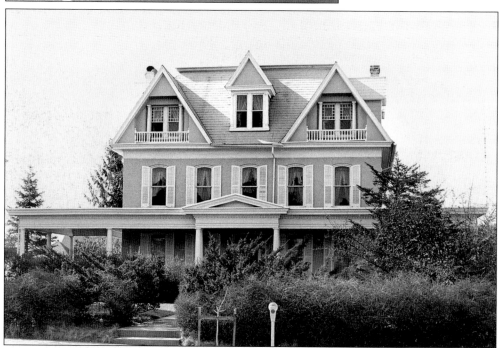

In 1872, Dr. John M. Ripple purchased a West Main Street lot where the former Western School had stood and built a large home. When his wife, Margaretta, went on vacation one year, he surprised her with a renovation that added a third floor with gables and dormers. The structure at 144 West Main Street was considered one of Waynesboro's finest residences in the late 19th century. (Courtesy of the Waynesboro Historical Society.)

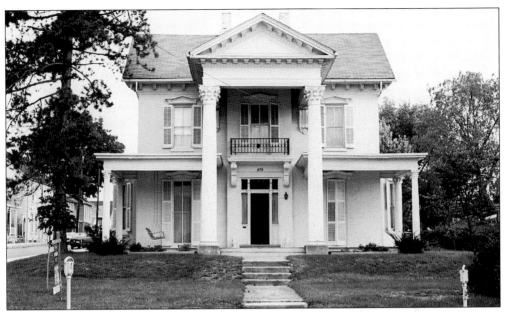

The Neoclassical J.H. Criswell house at 155 West Main Street was built in 1881 by William H. Snyder, who came to Waynesboro to learn the machinist's trade under George Frick. He became a master mechanic and was elected vice president of Frick in 1904. In 1902, he gave the house to his daughter, Anna Belle, who married dentist John Criswell, for whom the property is named. (Courtesy of the Waynesboro Historical Society.)

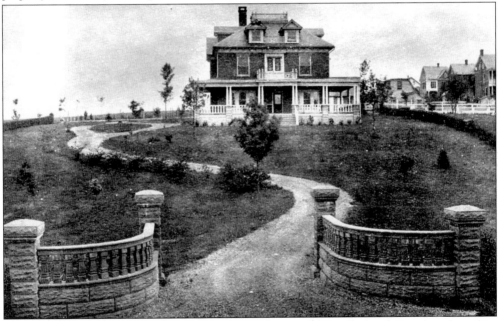

The home of Ferdinand Forthman at South Potomac and West Seventh Streets reflected its owner's status as one of Waynesboro's most prominent citizens in the last half of the 19th century. A successful druggist, Forthman served on the boards of many companies and was active in local fraternal organizations. The house, now without the elaborate entryway and carriage path, is still a private residence. (Courtesy of the Waynesboro Historical Society.)

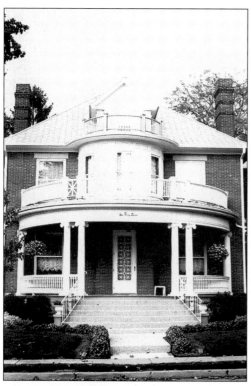

The Gilbert House on West King Street was built in 1908 by Lloyd Gilbert, a superintendent at Frick Company. The Colonial Revival house is nearly identical to an *American Homes* pattern published by a Tennessee architect, featuring a semicircular porch and upper porch balustrades. The slate roof was replaced with asphalt shingles in 1970, and the wooden steps were replaced with stone in 1990. (Courtesy of the Waynesboro Historical Society.)

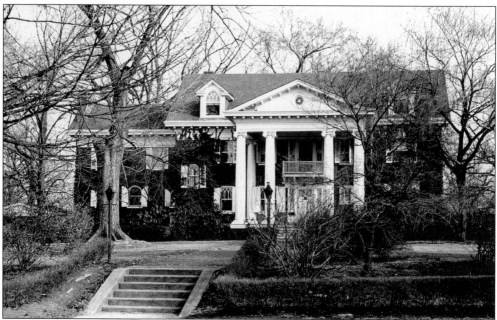

The Neoclassical A.O. Frick House at the northeast corner of Clayton Avenue and East Fifth Street was completed in 1906 for Abraham O. Frick, son of Frick Company founder George Frick. With its massive Ionic columns and separate five-bay and three-bay wings, the house reflects Waynesboro's increasing affluence in the early 1900s. (Courtesy of the Waynesboro Historical Society.)

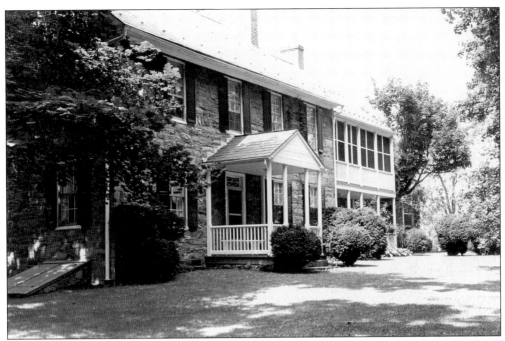

The stone residence of the Edgar Allen and Emma K. (Geiser) Nicodemus is the centerpiece of the beautiful Renfrew Museum and Park grounds located just east of Waynesboro. The house was built in 1812 by Daniel Royer. This 1973 photograph by W.J. "Wib" Davis was taken shortly after it was announced that Emma K. Nicodemus had willed the property to the Borough of Waynesboro. (Courtesy of the Waynesboro Historical Society.)

A winter snowfall gives the historic Welty's Mill Bridge a look straight out of a Currier and Ives print. The double-arch stone bridge was completed in 1856 by local builder David S. Stoner. The sturdy span handled automobile traffic until the late 1980s, when it was abandoned for a bridge built nearby. (Courtesy of the Waynesboro Historical Society.)

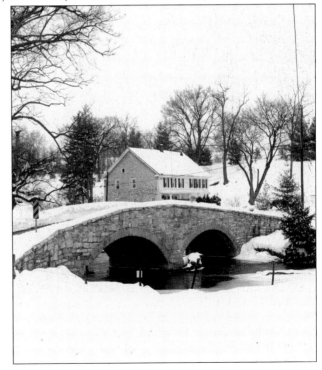

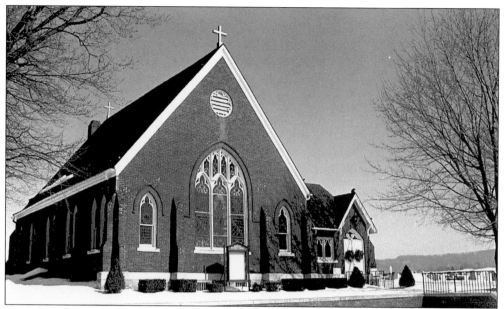

Harbaugh Reformed Church was built in 1892 in honor of Dr. Henry Harbaugh (1817–1867), a noted theologian who grew up on a farmstead near the Maryland state line south of Rouzerville. The Church of the Apostles eventually sold the unheated church to the Waynesboro Historical Society for $1. It is used for weddings, funerals, nondenominational services, and special programs. (Courtesy of the Waynesboro Historical Society.)

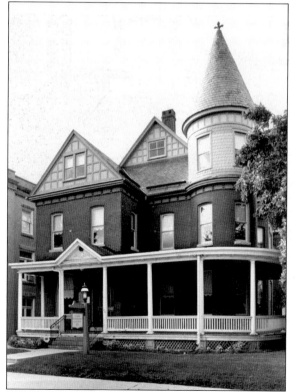

Oller House, at 138 West Main Street, is an example of Queen Anne–style Victorian architecture. It was built in 1892 by prominent Waynesboro businessman Joseph J. Oller. Oller's prosperity is reflected in the details and chestnut woodwork of the house. Oller's daughter, Rello, was born in the house in 1895 and bequeathed it to the Waynesboro Historical Society upon her death in 1992. (Courtesy of the Waynesboro Historical Society.)

Four
FACES OF WAYNESBORO

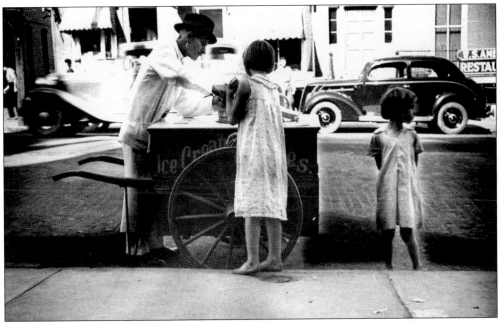

John Rossi scoops ice-cream treats for two youngsters in 1937. Born in Italy in 1870, Rossi was one of Waynesboro's most well-known street vendors and a favorite of town children. He sold 1¢ and 5¢ cones and 2¢ ice-cream sandwiches he made with a special metal mold. During cold-weather months, he worked at the Geiser Manufacturing Company. (Courtesy of Sylvester Snyder.)

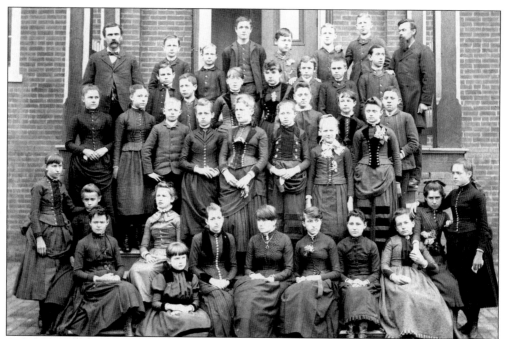

A well-dressed group of students lines the front steps of the Second Street School in this *c.* 1890s photograph. Second Street School, built in 1872, was Waynesboro's first high school. This photograph was saved by Mary Amberson, sixth from the left in the first row of standing students, who would later teach at Waynesboro High School. (Courtesy of the Waynesboro Historical Society.)

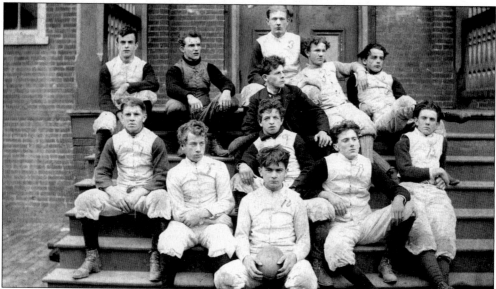

A tough-looking bunch of Waynesboro football players is seated on the steps of the Second Street School in 1892. In the front row, from left to right, are Jesse Beard, Dave Russell, Gurney Amberson (upper middle), Jake Zook (lower middle), Nevin Dietrich, and Clarence Beard. In the back row, from left to right, are Erle Hoke, Frank Good, Dave Zook (upper middle), Arthur Frantz (lower middle), Ed Hess, and Ed Miller. (Courtesy of the Waynesboro Historical Society.)

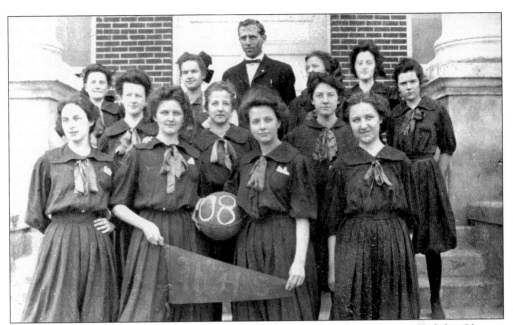

The 1908 Waynesboro high school girls' basketball team stands on the steps of the Clayton Avenue School, which was the high school at that time. This team was one of the first, if not the first, Waynesboro girls' team. (Courtesy of the Waynesboro Historical Society.)

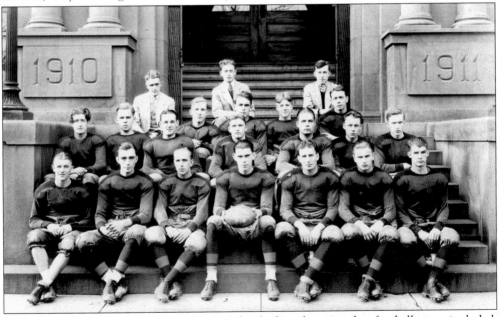

The 1927 Waynesboro High Tornado, the school's first championship football team, included, from left to right, the following: (first row) Chet Yingst, Harold Rowe, Lamar Sulanke, Raymond Smith, Cletus Bowers, Raymond Yingling, and Charles Snyder; (second row) John Strite, Daniel Long, W.J. "Wib" Davis, Carl Freeman, John Welty, Joe Fullerton, and Robert Pilkington; (third row) David Baker, Joseph Steiner, Francis Price, and Earl Webb; (fourth row) coach Percy E. "Pep" Probst, John Rowe, and Gerald McKelvey. (Courtesy of the Waynesboro Historical Society.)

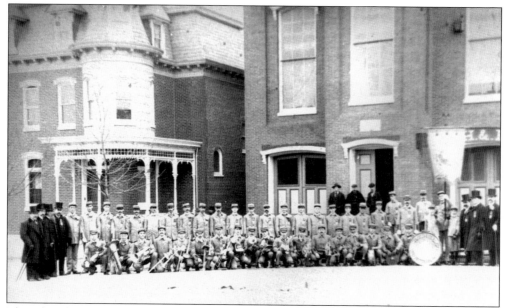

The Always There Hook and Ladder Company band lines up in front of the Academy of Music (borough hall), which served as the fire station during the last two decades of the 19th century. Mechanics Steam Fire Engine and Hose Company No. 1 occupied the west part of the building, and the Always There Hook and Ladder Company was in the east. The men in top hats are borough council members. (Courtesy of the Robert Ringer family.)

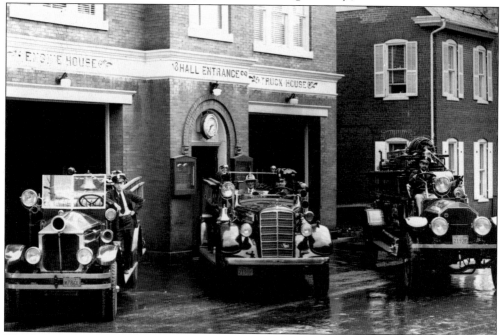

Waynesboro firefighters display their equipment at the old South Potomac Street fire hall in the early 1940s. From left to right are Jess Byers in a 1927 LaFrance community pumper (Waynesboro's first community pumper), Chief Bill Musey and Ken Lemmon in a 1941 Mack 505 pumper, and Mr. Lesher in a 1927 Ward-LaFrance truck. (Courtesy of the Robert Ringer family.)

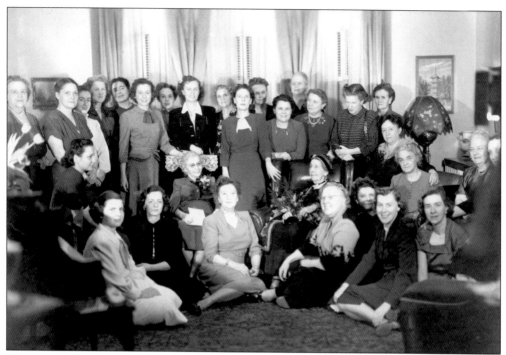

Women of the Euterpe Club gathered for this *c.* 1940s photograph. Organized as a music appreciation and performance club, the Euterpe is Waynesboro's oldest music club, dating from February 1910. (Courtesy of the Robert Ringer family.)

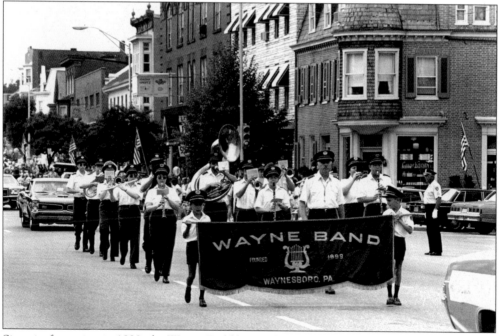

Since its formation in 1899, the Wayne Band has performed at hundreds of ceremonies, concerts, and parades in the Waynesboro area. Here, longtime director Asher Edelman marches at the head of the band in a 1970s-era Fourth of July parade. (Courtesy of Sid Miller, the *Record Herald.*)

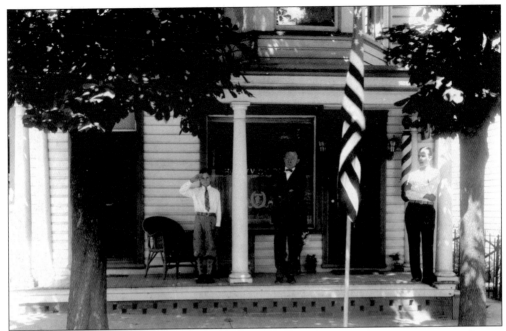

Earl O. Blair, 12, salutes the U.S. flag as it passes the Fritz Barber Shop, at 129 East Main Street, during the 1928 Fourth of July parade. Shop owner Harvey Fritz, center, and another barber to his right watch the parade. Blair served with distinction in the navy in World War II, participating in the Normandy invasion and South Pacific battles. (Courtesy of John Blair.)

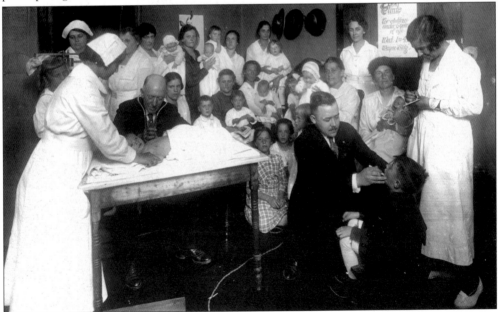

Dr. Robert B. Brown, shown on the right examining a child during a 1930s-era baby clinic in the Wayne Building, was one of Waynesboro's most popular and well-known citizens of the mid-20th century. A World War I veteran, "Doc" Brown served as Waynesboro mayor from 1950 to 1974, the longest term in borough history, after an earlier 1942–1946 stint as burgess. (Courtesy of the Robert Ringer family.)

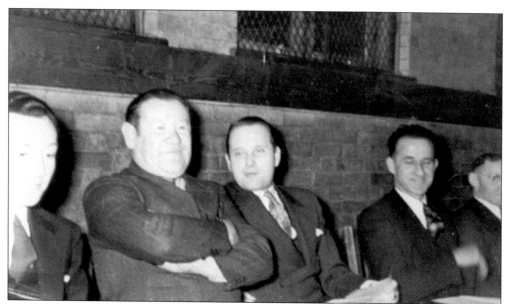

The Waynesboro YMCA lined up a special speaker for its February 28, 1941, Father-Son Banquet with Jim Thorpe, the legendary Carlisle Indian, making an appearance. From left to right are Irving Stoner, Thorpe, Roland Weaver, Art Kohler, and Jimmy Curran. (Courtesy of the Robert Ringer family.)

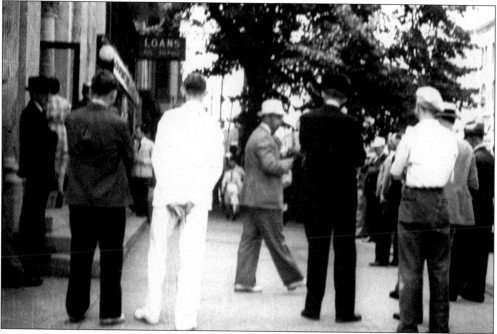

Auctioneer Leslie A. Bohn, wearing a white hat, offers stock for sale at the "Waynesboro Curb" in 1937. Common and preferred stock of local industries and banks were offered for years at these sales on Center Square. As large conglomerates started absorbing the Waynesboro companies, their stocks moved to the Big Board in New York, squelching this unique Waynesboro tradition. (Courtesy of Sylvester Snyder.)

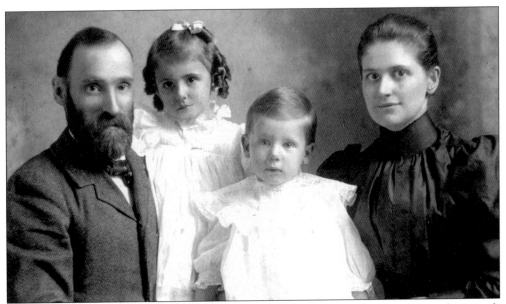

Waynesboro industrialist and philanthropist Joseph J. Oller sat for this late-1890s photograph with his wife, Myrtle (Funk) Oller; daughter, Rello; and son, J.F. The son of prominent local businessman Jacob F. Oller, Joseph Oller served as president of the Bank of Waynesboro and Landis Machine Company. He was one of the men behind the building of the Chambersburg, Greencastle, and Waynesboro Street Railway. (Courtesy of the Waynesboro Historical Society.)

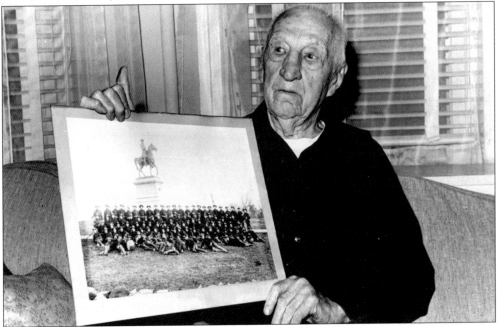

William S. Amberson was the last surviving Waynesboro veteran of the Spanish-American War. He is holding a picture of his unit—Company M, 5th Pennsylvania Volunteers. Amberson volunteered in July 1898, but the war ended before he saw action. "Mr. Will" died November 3, 1983, only a few days short of his 106th birthday. His father, Dr. J. Burns Amberson, had lived to age 98. (Courtesy of the Waynesboro Historical Society.)

One of Waynesboro's prominent early citizens, Gen. James Bourns (also spelled Burns) sat for this 1850 photograph with his grandson, James Burns Amberson. A captain in the War of 1812, Burns was called "General" because of his long association with the Pennsylvania militia. He served as sheriff of Franklin County and a justice of the peace. He owned the site where Burns Hill Cemetery was located and was the first person buried there. (Courtesy of the Waynesboro Historical Society.)

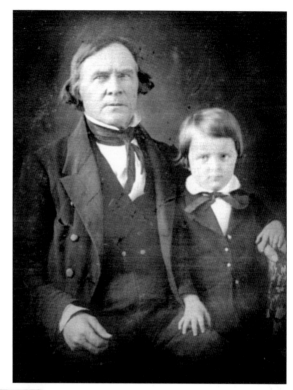

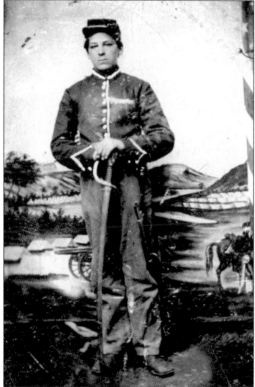

Zachary Taylor Funk proudly wears his Union uniform at the end of the Civil War in 1865. Capt. John E. Walker was the first volunteer from Waynesboro and served with distinction in the Union army until he was killed at Atlanta on August 5, 1864. His body was never recovered, but a cenotaph in Burns Hill Cemetery is inscribed in his honor. (Courtesy of the Waynesboro Historical Society.)

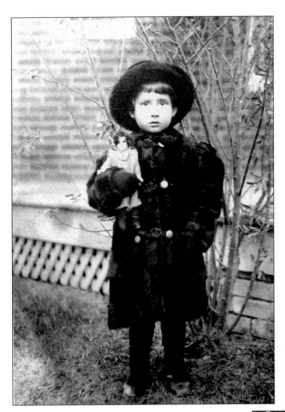

Sylvester Snyder, many of whose photographs grace this book, was a boy of four when this picture was taken in 1912. "I wanted to create images that would be of historic value some day . . . to document everyday life and special events so that future generations could see the way things used to be," Snyder has said. (Courtesy of Sylvester Snyder.)

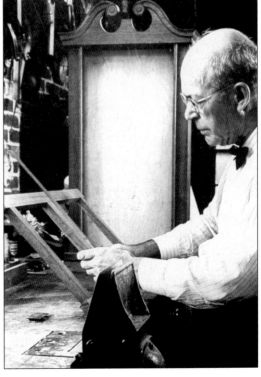

Amos P. Steiner, checking his work on a clock frame in this 1942 photograph, was one of Waynesboro's leading machinists in the early 20th century. He came to Waynesboro from Ohio in 1898 and became superintendent and chief engineer at Landis Tool Company. Steiner was highly regarded by his peers, and his death on January 8, 1945, was widely mourned. (Courtesy of Sylvester Snyder.)

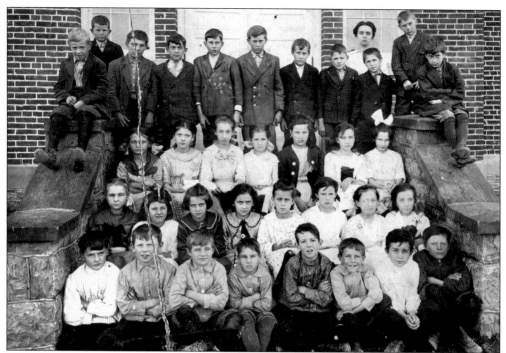

Aleta E. Wiles, fifth from the left in the third row, is the only student that can be identified in this *c.* 1913 photograph of Zullinger Elementary School students. Opened in 1911, the school was closed following the 1961–1962 school year and then served as the Zullinger Community Center before it was abandoned. A Waynesboro Historical Society project to renovate the building is under way. (Courtesy of Donald M. Ringer.)

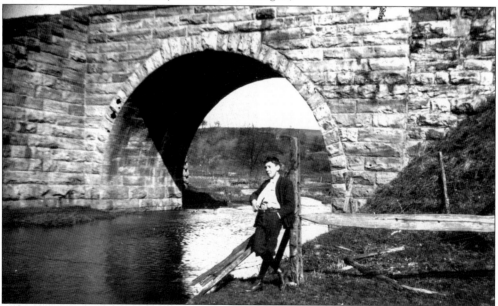

William R. Beckner is the pensive young man standing near the Baltimore and Cumberland Valley Railroad viaduct near Price's Church in this *c.* 1905 photograph. (Courtesy of the Waynesboro Historical Society.)

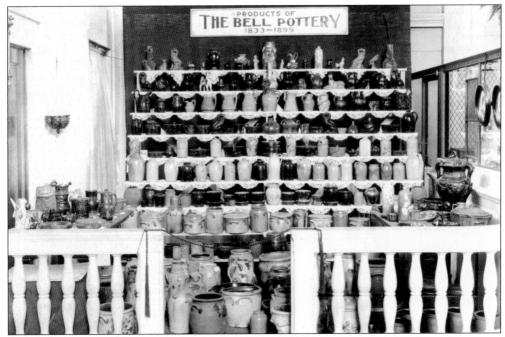

Over 250 pieces of pottery produced by the plant of local artisan John Bell, whose plant was a Waynesboro landmark from 1833 to 1899, were displayed at the First National Bank of Waynesboro in 1925. Local red, white, and gray clays were used to make the pottery, which is highly prized by collectors today. Bell's plant was located near what is now the intersection of West Main and Potomac Streets. (Courtesy of the First National Bank and Trust Company.)

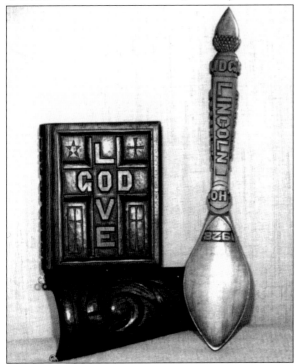

Itinerant carver Frank Feather walked the rural roads of Franklin County, Pennsylvania, and Washington County, Maryland, for nearly a half-century. In return for lodging, food, or a fee, Feather, who died in 1951, created exquisitely carved hardwood canes, spoons, sconces—even the wooden "Bible" shown in this photograph. One of Feather's canes recently sold for $5,900 at auction. (Courtesy of Shawn Meyers.)

Patrolman William Daywalt, father of five sons, was killed in a gunfight involving two drunken brothers, Abe and Bill Barnes, on February 4, 1914. After words were exchanged at Center Square, a running battle ensued, and Abe Barnes shot Daywalt at the Edward Hess farm near town. Abe was later killed by a state constable. Bill surrendered and was jailed. Daywalt remains the only Waynesboro policeman killed in the line of duty. (Courtesy of the Borough of Waynesboro.)

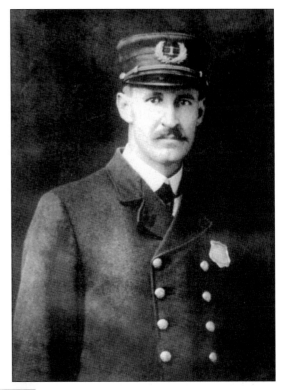

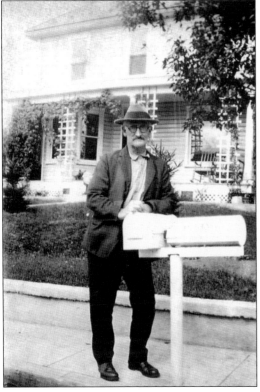

William Otha Ringer removed the rural mailbox in front of his house at 27 Roadside Avenue in 1938 as city delivery began at his address. Ringer served as superintendent of Burns Hill Cemetery, worked at local businesses, and was the Clayton Avenue School janitor for 22 years, where many students knew him as "Pappy." He retired in 1940 and died at home at age 77 in 1943. (Courtesy of Donald M. Ringer.)

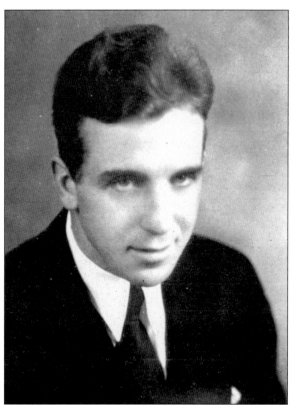

Charles A. "Rip" Engle, a native of Elk Lick (now Salisbury), was the most successful high school football coach in Waynesboro history. He came to Waynesboro from Western Maryland College in 1930 and led the Blue and Gold Tornado to a 76-21-7 record before leaving to take an assistant coaching job at Western Maryland in 1941. (Courtesy of the Waynesboro Historical Society.)

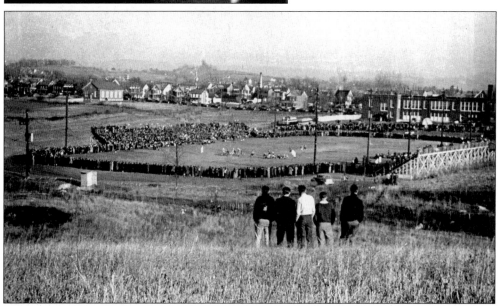

More than 6,000 fans were on hand to watch the Waynesboro Blue and Gold Tornado defeat Hagerstown 8-0 in the 1939 Thanksgiving Day game at School Stadium, located behind the Fairview Avenue School. Coach "Rip" Engle's squad had a 9-0 record that season and outscored its opponents 192-6. Engle, later coach at Penn State, had three unbeaten squads during his 1930–1940 Waynesboro tenure. (Courtesy of Sylvester Snyder.)

74

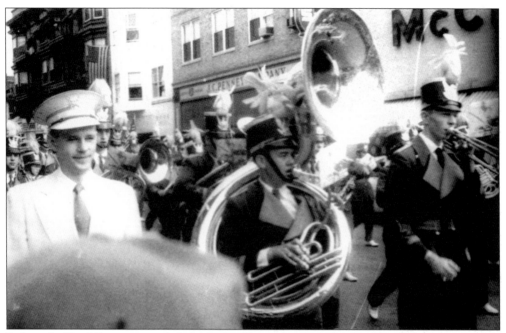

Robert A. "Raz" Zimmerman, left, leads the Waynesboro High School band on a march down Main Street in this *c.* 1950s shot. The popular Zimmerman directed the band from 1950 to 1974. (Courtesy of Sylvester Snyder.)

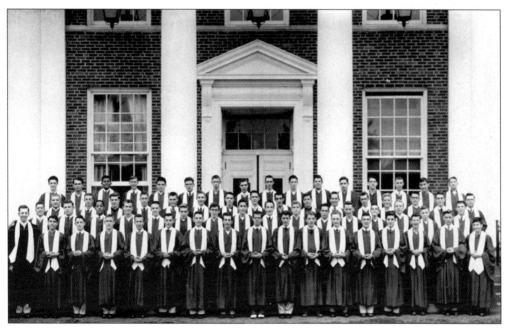

Under the direction of Francis Nogle and later, for many years, Gerald Kowallis, the Tribesmen became a popular choral fixture at Waynesboro High School. This is the first group of Tribesmen on the steps of East Junior High, then the high school, in 1955. (Courtesy of the Robert Ringer family.)

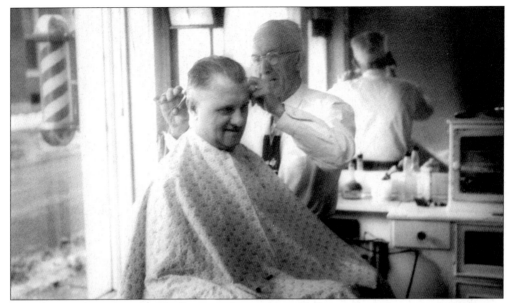

Woodrow Wilson "Dutch" Shaffer, seen here giving Chalmers Cordell a trim in 1960, was known for both boxing and barbering in Waynesboro. A professional fighter of some note as a youth, Shaffer later trained fighters and promoted bouts at area fairs and festivals in the 1930s and 1940s. He was also active in church and civic affairs. (Courtesy of Sylvester Snyder.)

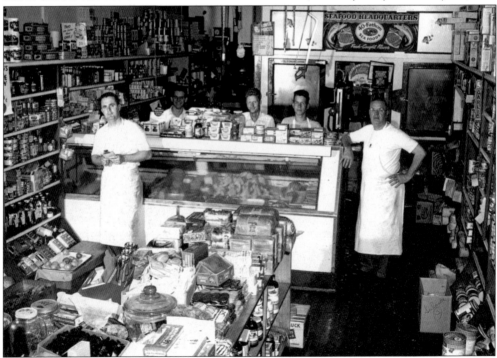

Sulanke's Meat Market was located at 35 East Main Street at the time of the 1947 sesquicentennial celebration in Waynesboro. Through the years, Waynesboro had dozens of neighborhood groceries, meat markets, and seafood stores. With competition from supermarkets and convenience chains, few remain nowadays. (Courtesy of the Waynesboro Historical Society.)

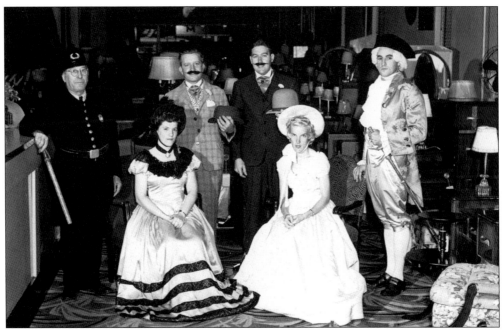

Dressed in 1947 sesquicentennial fashion garb at Miller's Furniture Store in downtown Waynesboro are, from left to right, Charles "Mac" McFerren, Gladys Kuhn Mentzer, William Wagner, Chauncy Blubaugh, Isabelle Smetzer, and Robert "Tip" Rowe. (Courtesy of the Waynesboro Historical Society.)

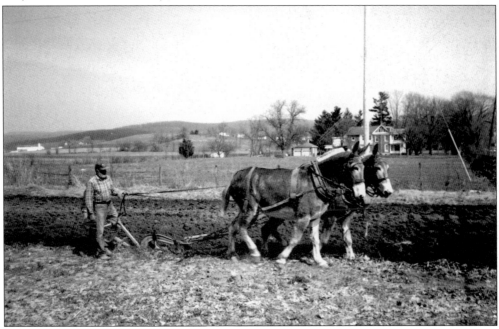

For years, visitors have come from as far away as Washington, D.C., to watch Herb Frantz plow his field the old-fashioned way—with mules—as he is doing in this 1996 photograph. Frantz has also raised Belgian horses on his White Hall Farm, located east of Waynesboro on Pennsylvania Route 16. (Courtesy of Donald M. Ringer.)

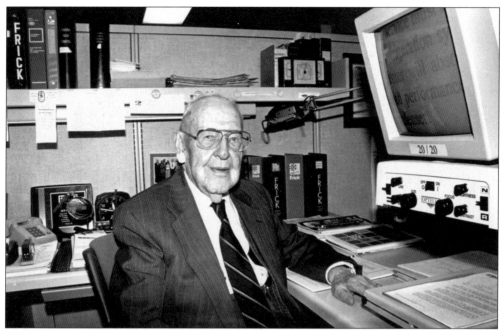

Former Frick Company vice president of engineering Milton W. Garland gained national attention as "America's oldest worker" in 1998. He was still reporting to the office daily at age 102, with the title of senior consultant of technical services. Known as "Mr. Refrigeration," Garland started with Frick in 1920 and held more than 40 patents. He passed away at age 104. (Courtesy of the Robert Ringer family.)

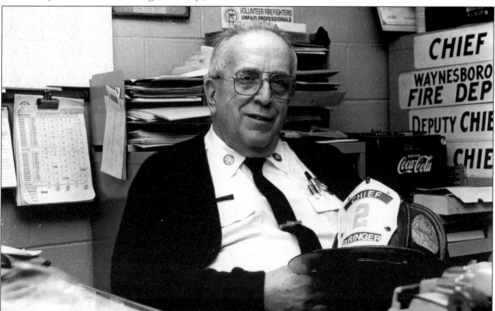

Donald M. Ringer served as Waynesboro's fire chief from 1990 to 1997. Like his brother, the late Robert L. Ringer, he is an avid local historian and an expert on the history of Waynesboro firefighting. He continues to serve Waynesboro as the borough's emergency management coordinator. (Courtesy of Sid Miller, the *Record Herald*.)

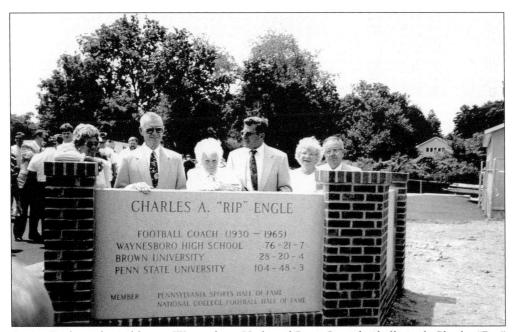

Sunny Engle, widow of former Waynesboro High and Penn State football coach Charles "Rip" Engle, observes a monument dedicated to her husband on July 23, 1995. The former Indian Stadium was renamed Engle Field on that day. Flanking Sunny Engle are Joseph Kugler, left, and Penn State coach Joe Paterno. (Courtesy of Donald M. Ringer.)

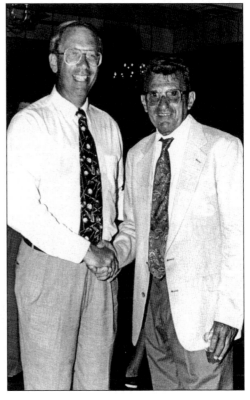

A football legend visited Waynesboro in 1995 as Penn State coach Joe Paterno, right, shakes hands with school superintendent Michael Moskalski. Paterno spoke at a ceremony to rename the high school's stadium Engle Field in honor of Charles A. "Rip" Engle, former Waynesboro and Penn State coach. Engle coached Paterno at Brown University and later hired him as an assistant at Penn State. (Courtesy of Sid Miller, the *Record Herald*.)

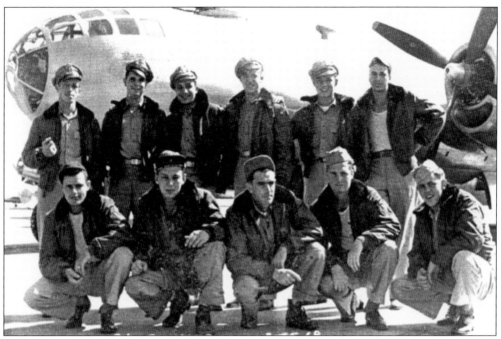

Lt. Guy L. Bonner of Waynesboro, the first man on the left in the top row, was reported missing in the Pacific theater with his entire B-29 crew in July 1945, shortly before the end of World War II. Bonner had served in the army for four and a half years. He was employed by Landis Tool Company in the engineering department before joining the service. (Courtesy of the Waynesboro Historical Society.)

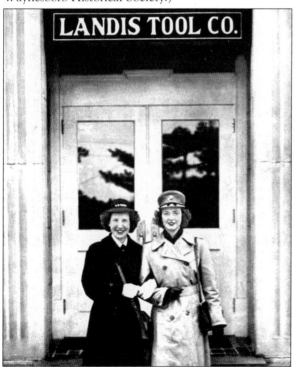

Waynesboro industries contributed to World War II through production and employees who joined the military. Here, S1c. Florence Beckner, left, and Marine S.Sgt. Mary Weagly visit the Landis Tool plant in 1945. Beckner had been employed in the cost department and Weagly was in the main office at Landis. (Courtesy of the Waynesboro Historical Society.)

Five
CELEBRATIONS
AND RECREATION

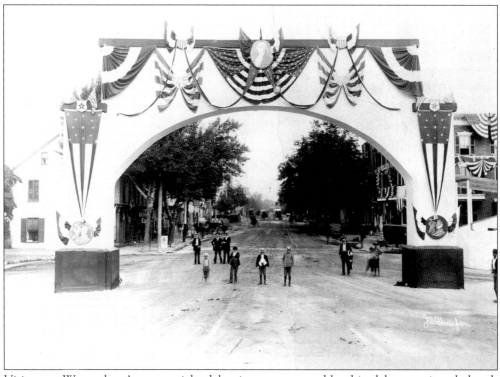

Visitors to Waynesboro's centennial celebration were greeted by this elaborate triumphal arch in Center Square. Parades and races passed under the massive arch. Gov. Daniel Hastings of Pennsylvania and Gov. Lloyd Lowndes of Maryland addressed the crowd in Center Square following the September 1, 1897, civic parade. (Courtesy of the Waynesboro Historical Society.)

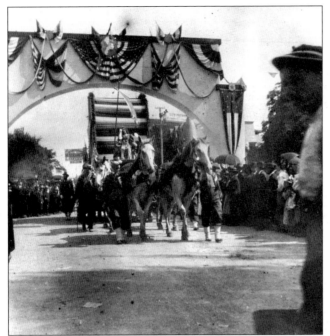

Drawn by four horses led by men in oriental costumes, the Geiser Manufacturing Company float passes through the centennial arch during the September 2, 1897, Trades Display parade. A major manufacturer of steam-powered engines, threshers, and sawmills, Geiser was in its peak years of success. (Courtesy of Sylvester Snyder.)

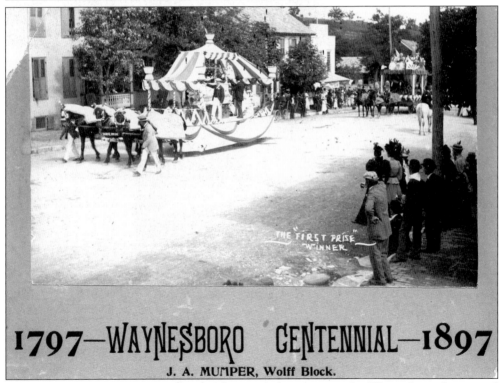

THE "FIRST PRIZE" WINNER

1797—WAYNESBORO CENTENNIAL—1897

J. A. MUMPER, Wolff Block.

The Mentzer and Clugston Drug Store float took first prize in the Waynesboro Centennial Trades Display parade on September 2, 1897. The Mentzer and Clugston store was located in the Shively Building at 5 West Main Street from 1893 to 1905. (Courtesy of the Waynesboro Historical Society.)

This float featuring a white swan surrounded by white-clad girls on a bed of white cotton was one of two entered by Good Brothers dry goods emporium in the Centennial Trades Display. It won second prize. The writer of the centennial souvenir program, who said no good photograph of the float existed, must not have been aware of this shot taken by an unknown photographer. (Courtesy of Sylvester Snyder.)

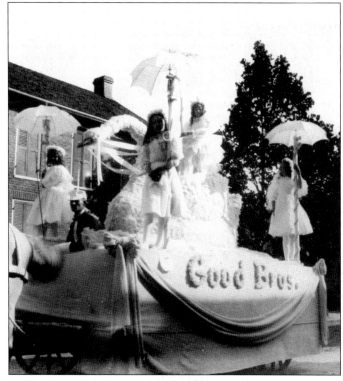

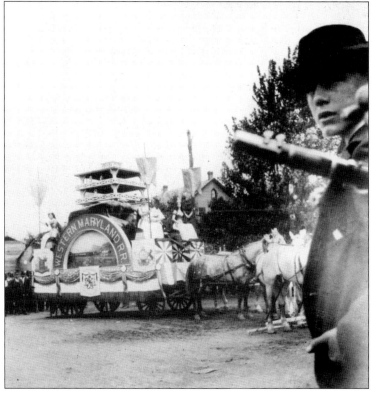

The "Allegorical Tableau Car" of the Western Maryland Railroad was considered one of the finest floats in the Waynesboro Centennial Trades Display parade. The float, constructed by railroad employees in the Union Bridge, Maryland, shops, featured four young ladies representing agriculture, science, mechanics, and commerce seated at the corners. A replica of the High Rock observatory crowned the float. (Courtesy of Sylvester Snyder.)

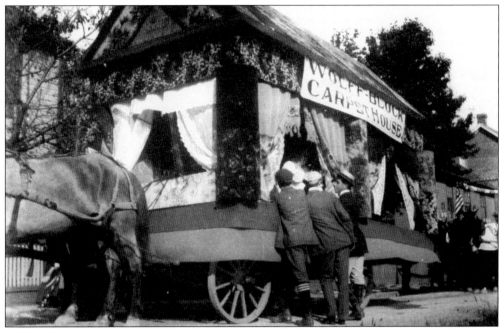

Some things never change. In this 1897 photograph, a group of young men strike up a conversation with some young ladies seated inside the Wolff Block Carpet House float that was entered in the Centennial Trades Display parade. Brothers James P. and John M. Wolff had moved their dry goods business into a new store at 26–30 East Main Street in 1893. (Courtesy of Sylvester Snyder.)

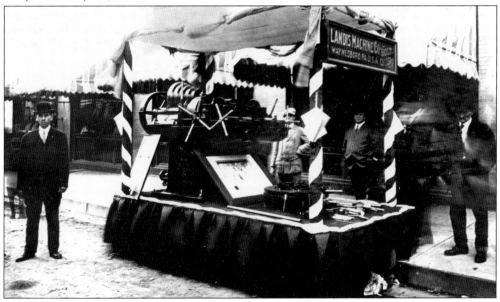

Farmer's Day, celebrated the first Saturday in October, was a big event in Waynesboro in the years just before the United States entered World War I. Exhibits lined Main Street, and there were races and contests of all kinds. This is the Landis Machine Company's exhibit at the 1913 Farmer's Day. The man standing to the left of the exhibit is Emery Heefner. (Courtesy of the Waynesboro Historical Society.)

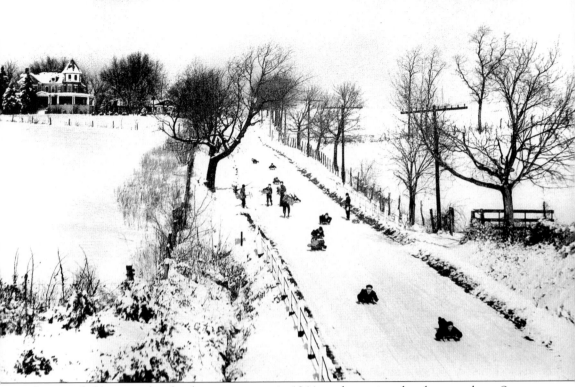

It was a sledding paradise for these youngsters in 1944, as they enjoyed a clear run down State Road Hill (Route 997) on the outskirts of Waynesboro. Bad weather and World War II gas rationing limited car traffic. The large house in the upper left was built by florist Henry Eichholz in 1908 and still stands on what was known as McDermott's Hill. (Courtesy of Sylvester Snyder.)

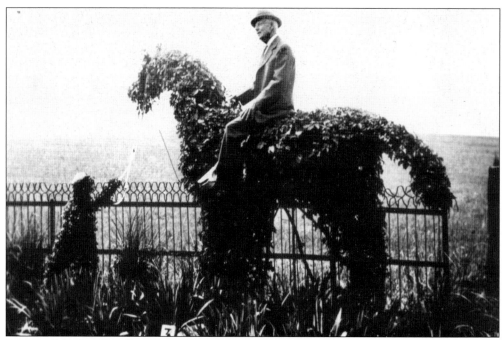

Ferdinand S. "Ferd" Gilbert created a topiary "zoo" in Waynesboro in the late 1920s and early 1930s along South Potomac Street south from Sixth Street. Gilbert was superintendent of Green Hill Cemetery and in charge of landscaping. His zoo was featured in postcards and newsreels that brought national attention, but his creations passed away with him in 1934. (Courtesy of the Waynesboro Historical Society.)

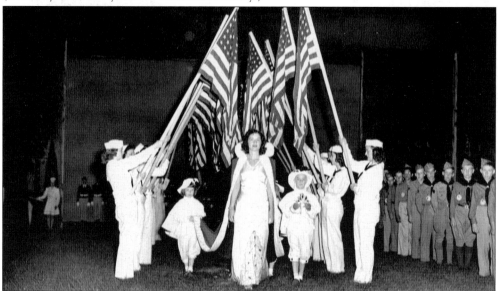

Gladys Stitely, who was Miss Waynesboro for the 1947 sesquicentennial, moves under an arch of flags at School Stadium during the finale to a presentation of the celebration's pageant "Crossroads Review." Approximately 1,000 local residents appeared in the pageant, which had a script authored by journalist W.J. "Wib" Davis. An estimated 15,000 people attended the five performances. (Courtesy of the Waynesboro Historical Society.)

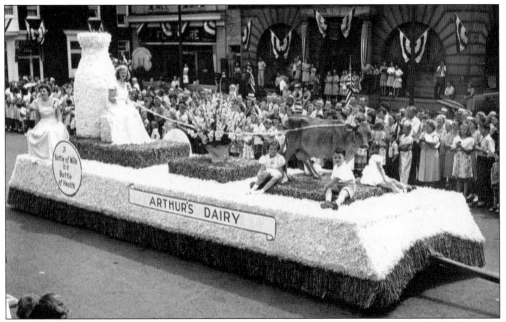

The Arthur's Dairy float passes through Center Square during the Waynesboro sesquicentennial civic parade on July 11, 1947. The Arthur's float won first prize in the parade's commercial division. (Courtesy of the Waynesboro Historical Society.)

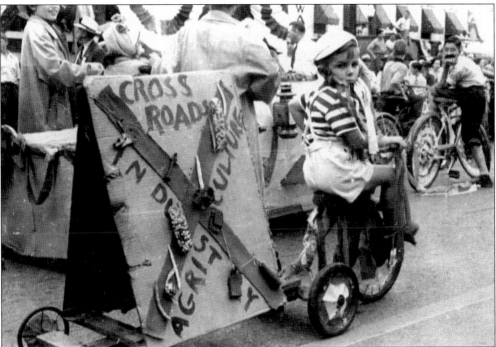

A youngster identified by photographer Sylvester Snyder as Kenny Monn prepares to ride his tricycle-powered "float" in the 1947 Waynesboro sesquicentennial youth parade. His sign reads "Crossroads of Agriculture and Industry," Waynesboro's motto that was used for the sesquicentennial. (Courtesy of Sylvester Snyder.)

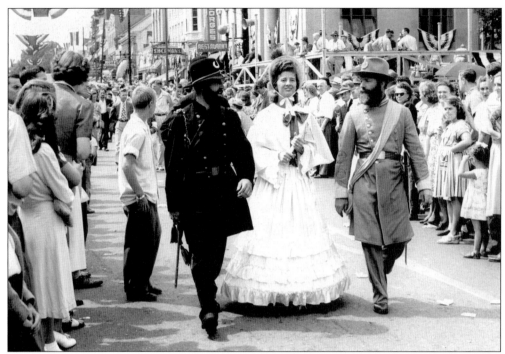

Charles Besecker, many of whose photographs are included in the huge collection of local historian Robert L. Ringer, was an avid recorder of Waynesboro events. His extensive portfolio of the 1947 sesquicentennial celebration included this shot of the fashion parade held on July 9. (Courtesy of the Waynesboro Historical Society.)

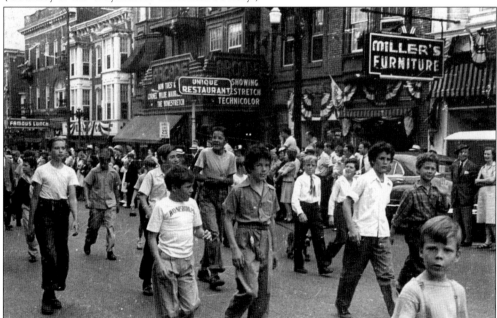

Waynesboro youths take over Main Street during the sesquicentennial youth parade of July 8, 1947. Decked in summer gear of the time, the kids stroll past Miller's Furniture, the Unique Restaurant, and the Arcade theater. (Courtesy of Sylvester Snyder.)

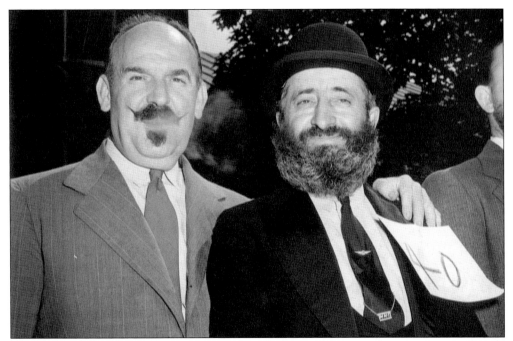

The Brothers of the Brush whisker club was formed for the 1947 sesquicentennial, and its beard-and moustache-growing contest, featuring more than 300 men, was a hit. Here, mustachioed Burgess (Mayor) Harry C. Funk, left, stands in line with beard contest entrant Merle Gilbert. Brothers of the Brush was revived for another sesquicentennial (of Waynesboro's incorporation as a borough) in 1968 and is still active. (Courtesy of the Waynesboro Historical Society.)

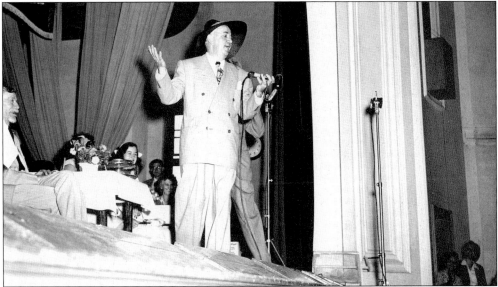

One of the highlights of the 1947 sesquicentennial for Waynesboro residents was the return of native son Tom Breneman. Breneman, a popular radio personality of the time, brought his entire "Breakfast in Hollywood" show from California to Waynesboro and broadcast all week from the high school auditorium. Every show drew a capacity crowd. (Courtesy of the Waynesboro Historical Society.)

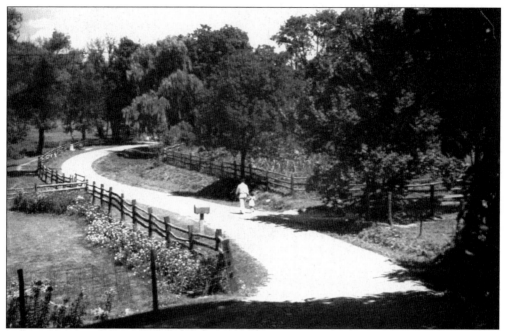

Sometimes the biggest pleasures in life are simple things, like a walk with your dad along a quiet country road. The is Lyons Road as it looked in 1941 in Washington Township. There is still rural beauty in the Waynesboro area, but most of the roads are not so quiet these days. (Courtesy of Sylvester Snyder.)

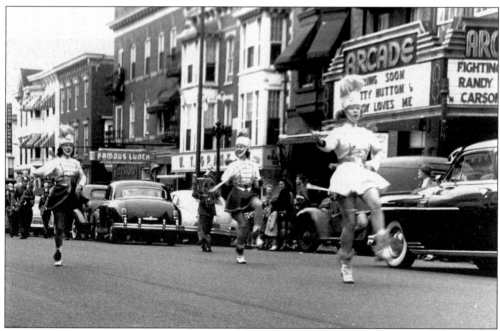

A trio of high-stepping majorettes lead the Waynesboro High School band in a parade down West Main Street in 1953. From left to right are Nancy Jones, Carole Ann Knupp, and Mary Lou Palmer. (Courtesy of the Robert Ringer family.)

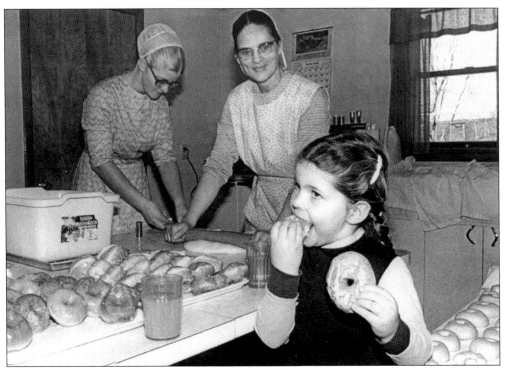

The heritage of Waynesboro's settlers of German descent comes to the fore on Shrove Tuesday, known locally as Fastnacht Day, which is similar to Fat Tuesday. Civic groups and bakeries traditionally produce dozens of treats, especially doughnuts, on the special day. For years, the Martin family on Hollowell Church Road made highly regarded doughnuts in their kitchen. (Courtesy of Sid Miller, the *Record Herald*.)

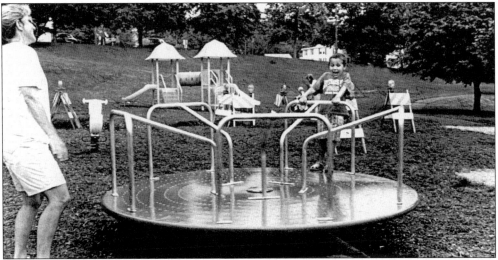

Waynesboro's centrally located Memorial Park has for decades been a place to stroll, play tennis, baseball, basketball, and other sports, or just plain relax. The park got its start in the mid-1940s, when the borough purchased the 4.6-acre site of E-B Field, the former location of the high school athletic grounds and a Blue Ridge League baseball diamond. (Courtesy of Sid Miller, the *Record Herald*.)

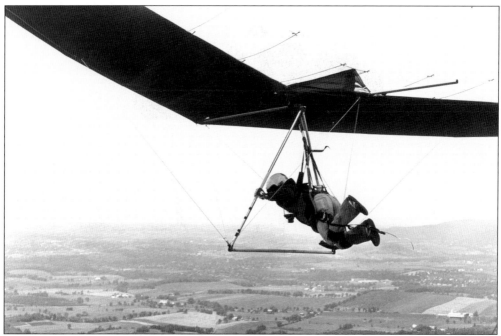

Although it is no longer the site of a once-popular observation platform, High Rock near Pen Mar Park has been a popular launching site with hang-gliding enthusiasts for years. Strong wind currents, high altitude, and a scenic view attract the gliders. Occasionally, gliders have become entangled on the side of the mountain, causing extra work for local fire and rescue companies. (Courtesy of Sid Miller, the *Record Herald*.)

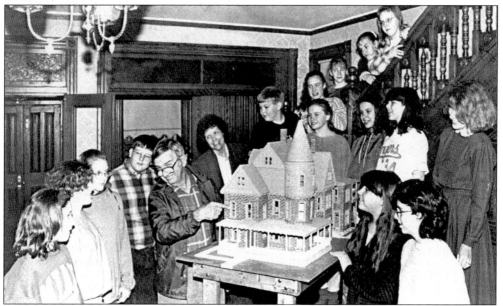

Jacob E. Beck shows off his elaborate handcrafted model of the Oller House, now the Waynesboro Historical Society headquarters, to an appreciative group of students at the Oller House. Beck has made several other models of local historic landmarks. (Courtesy of Sid Miller, the *Record Herald*.)

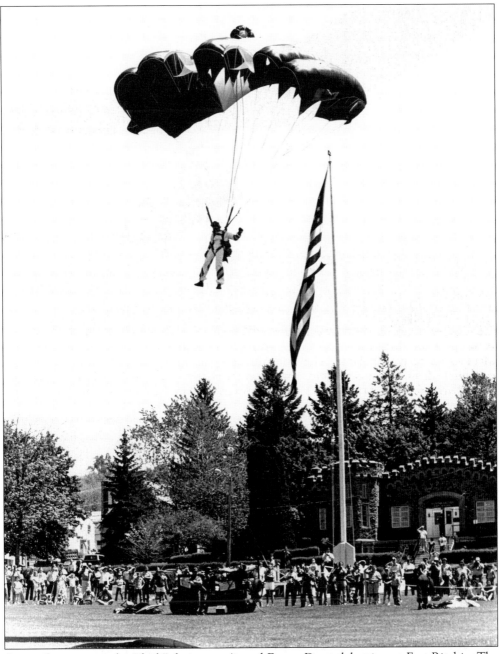

A parachutist nears the "deck" during an Armed Forces Day celebration at Fort Ritchie. The fort, just over the border from Pennsylvania in Cascade, Maryland, was a center for the Army Signal Corps. With a scenic location and great recreational facilities, it was considered a good posting. Washington County, Maryland, officials presently are trying to determine how to develop the fort, which the military has vacated. (Courtesy of Sid Miller, the *Record Herald*.)

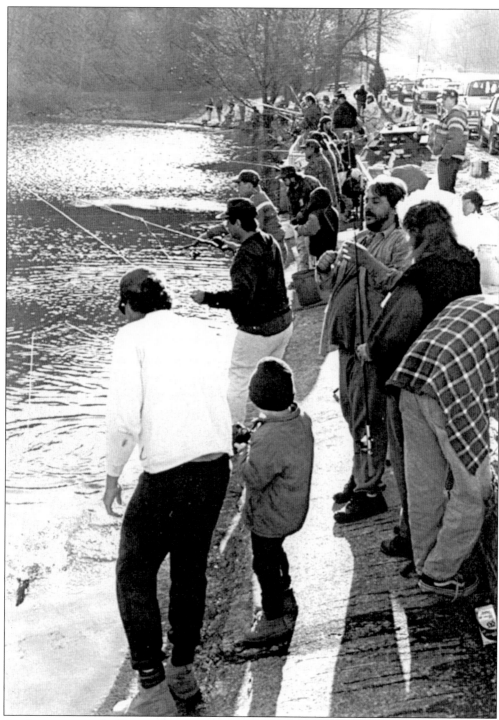

Anglers young and old cast their lines in a fishing rodeo at Red Run Park in Washington Township. Work on the park started in August 1938 under the sponsorship of the borough of Waynesboro, which received a $52,000 Works Progress Administration appropriation for the project and $2,000 from individual subscribers. (Courtesy of Sid Miller, the *Record Herald*.)

Six
NOTEWORTHY EVENTS

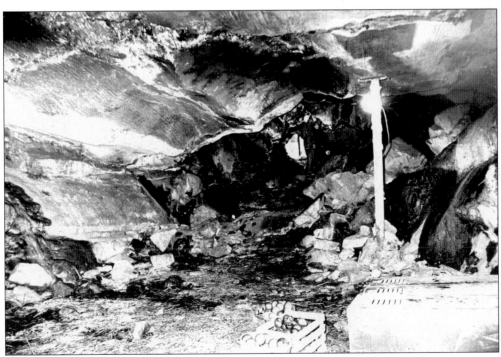

Needy's Cave, located along Falls Creek near Shank's Mill on Amsterdam Road, was a stop on the Underground Railroad used by slaves fleeing the south before the Civil War. It also has provided a cool place for the Needy family and their successors to store food, as shown by the apples in this view. Several Underground Railroad sites were located in the Waynesboro area. (Courtesy of Becky Dietrich.)

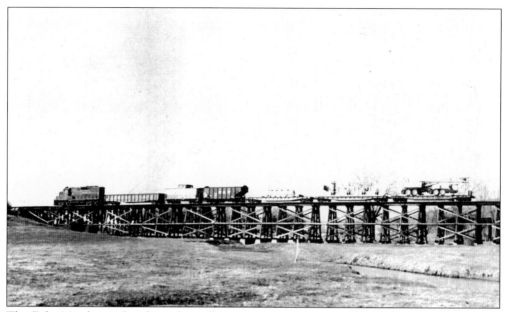

The Foltz Meadow railroad trestle, well known to generations of Waynesboro area residents, was built shortly after the Baltimore and Cumberland Valley Railroad Extension Company started an extension to Chambersburg in 1880. The trestle's dismantling by the Chessie System in 1985 effectively marked the end of Waynesboro's 100-year era of railroad access. (Courtesy of the Robert Ringer family.)

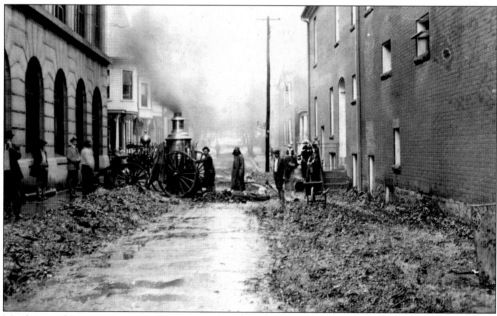

Mechanics fire company members use a Nott steam pumper to remove water from the Bank of Waynesboro cellar on South Church Street after the hailstorm of June 6, 1917. The storm caused extensive cellar flooding, and baseball-sized hail broke thousands of windows in the borough. The Emerson-Brantingham Company shops alone had between 20,000 and 25,000 panes of glass broken. (Courtesy of the Waynesboro Historical Society.)

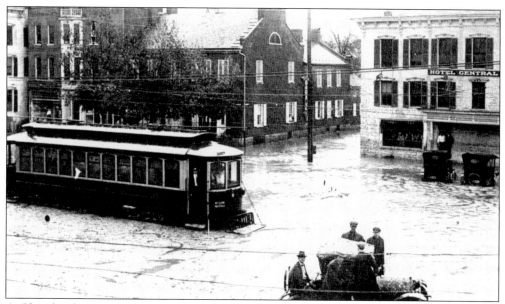

A Chambersburg, Greencastle, and Waynesboro trolley car is stranded along with a group of motorists in Center Square during the fierce storm of June 6, 1917. Torrential rain and hail clogged sewers, flooding the square to a depth of two feet and soaking merchandise in the cellars of nearby stores. (Courtesy of the Waynesboro Historical Society.)

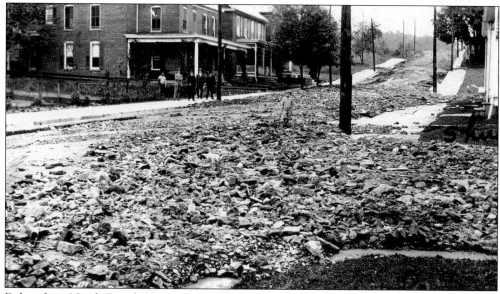

Debris from North Broad Street piled up at the intersection with East North Street during the storm of June 6, 1917. The storm caused an estimated $100,000 in damage—a huge amount at the time—in Waynesboro. About 70,000 square feet of glass were sold the day after the storm. Several additional carloads of glass were ordered to repair hail damage. (Courtesy of the Waynesboro Historical Society.)

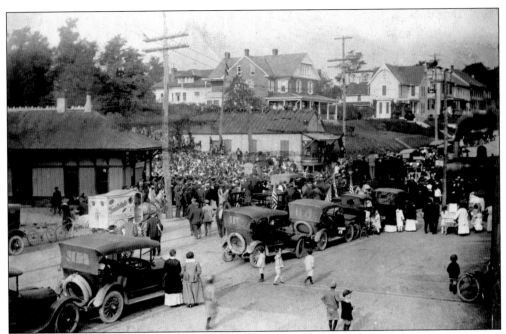

On September 20, 1917, an estimated 3,000 people gathered to see 77 World War I draftees depart from the Western Maryland depot. Locally, Waynesboro's Charles E. Shoemaker held the first number, 258, drawn in the draft. The men assembled in Center Square before marching west on Main Street to the station; they were followed by Civil War veterans, firemen, and many automobiles. (Courtesy of the Robert Ringer family.)

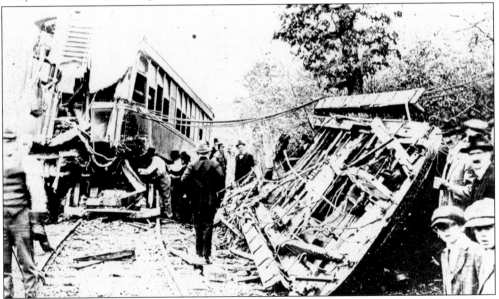

On May 22, 1920, popular Greencastle, Chambersburg, and Waynesboro Street Railway general manager R.D. Sefton was killed in this wreck at the foot of the grade between Pen Mar and Rouzerville. Sefton was returning to Waynesboro in a three-car train when the brakes failed and the train plowed into a car ahead. Although 10 other people were seriously injured, Sefton was the only fatality. (Courtesy of Becky Dietrich.)

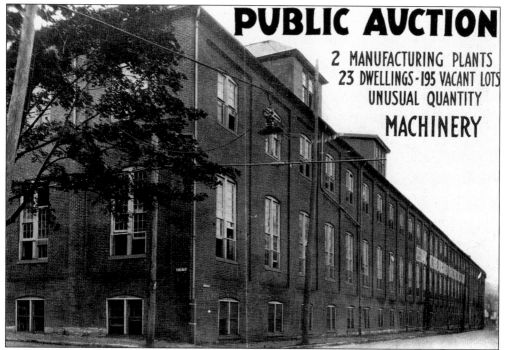

PUBLIC AUCTION
2 MANUFACTURING PLANTS
23 DWELLINGS-195 VACANT LOTS
UNUSUAL QUANTITY
MACHINERY

When the Emerson-Brantingham Company hit financial trouble, it was decided to auction off the former Geiser Manufacturing Company assets in 1925, including this 334-foot-long building at East Second and South Broad Streets. A group of local investors raised enough money to purchase the plant and continue production, but the Great Depression finished off Geiser in the 1930s. (Courtesy of the Waynesboro Historical Society.)

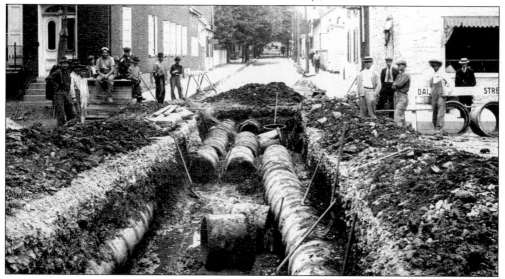

A federal Works Progress Administration grant enabled Waynesboro to build a sanitary sewer system in the 1930s. This crew is putting in a line at Main and North Church Streets in Center Square in 1934. Borough residents were shocked on July 6, 1934, when a hand-dug sewer trench on Philadelphia Avenue collapsed, killing sewer project workers George Mundy, George Hartman, and Charles Miller. (Courtesy of the Robert Ringer family.)

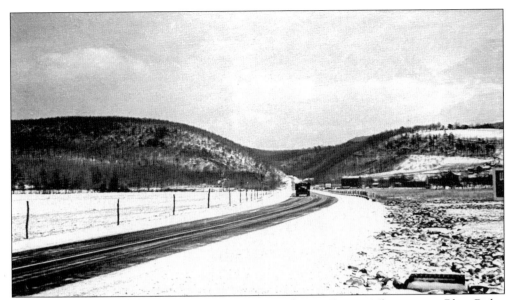

The construction of the "Sunshine Trail" (Pennsylvania Route 16) route to Blue Ridge Summit, beginning in 1937, was a big improvement over the old Route 16, a winding road that led from Rouzerville up the mountain and was prone to icing and snow drifts during the winter. Here, a lone truck descends a then-undeveloped stretch of the new road in 1939. (Courtesy of Sylvester Snyder.)

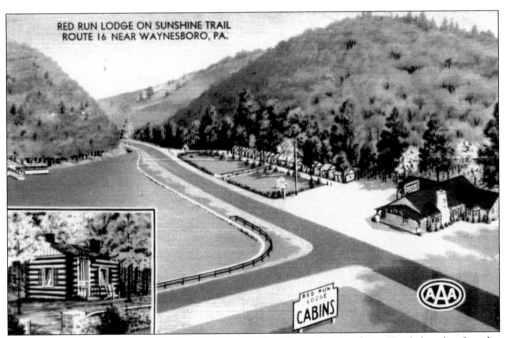

RED RUN LODGE ON SUNSHINE TRAIL
ROUTE 16 NEAR WAYNESBORO, PA.

CABINS

AAA

Local orchardist Ike Smith built the Red Run Lodge along the Sunshine Trail shortly after the road's completion in 1939. The lodge and its once-spiffy guest cabins can still be seen today but are in a badly deteriorated condition. (Courtesy of the Robert Ringer family.)

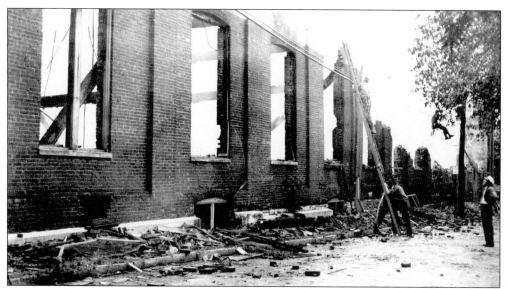

Wilmer Shifflet, right, of Mechanics Steam Fire Engine and Hose Company looks on as men check the smoldering remains of the Geiser Manufacturing Company complex. Fire hit the abandoned plant on August 24, 1940, and destroyed most of the company's site, which amounted to about four square blocks of Waynesboro. (Courtesy of the Waynesboro Historical Society.)

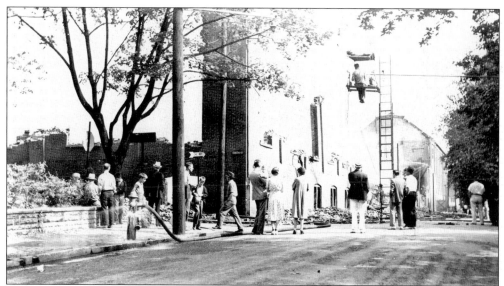

Curious onlookers at the intersection of East Second and South Broad Streets examine the ruins of the Geiser Manufacturing plant following the August 24, 1940, fire. The fire is believed to have been caused by a smoldering welding torch left behind by a worker who was removing old equipment from the plant. It was a sad finale for a company with a history dating back to the mid-1860s. (Courtesy of the Waynesboro Historical Society.)

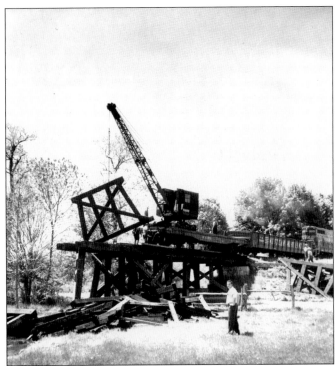

Chessie System workers dismantle the trestle off Price's Church Road in 1985. The trestle was part of the Baltimore and Cumberland Valley extension to Chambersburg started in the 1880s for the Western Maryland Railroad. The arrival of the automobile ended passenger service, and trucking made local freight operations impractical. Waynesboro, which had eagerly sought a railroad 105 years earlier, was without service again. (Courtesy of Brian Sease.)

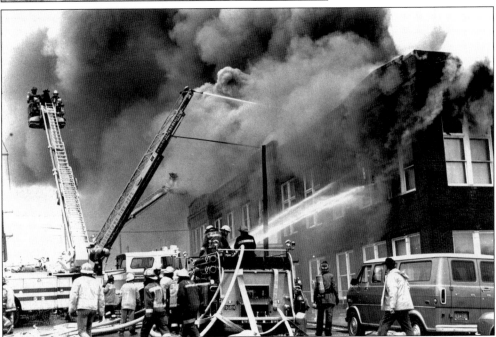

The nine-alarm Frick Company office fire on November 19, 1988, caused between $3 and $4 million in damage. A total of 250 firefighters from at least 25 fire companies and 5 counties fought the blaze. False ceilings placed in the building over the years hampered their efforts. The fire was ruled an act of arson, and an arrest was made five years later, but charges were dropped. (Courtesy of Sid Miller, the *Record Herald*.)

Seven

MONT ALTO AND QUINCY

These stereoscopic cards depict the Mont Alto iron ore furnace and the Mont Alto Park railroad station platform. The Mont Alto Railroad was built in 1872 to transport products of the furnace. By 1875, the park was ready for recreation, and the train served two purposes. On some days, as many as 7,000 to 8,000 people came to the park by train. (Courtesy of Becky Dietrich.)

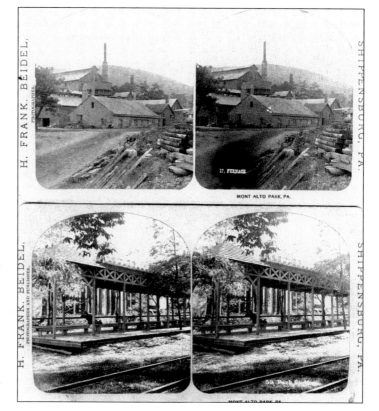

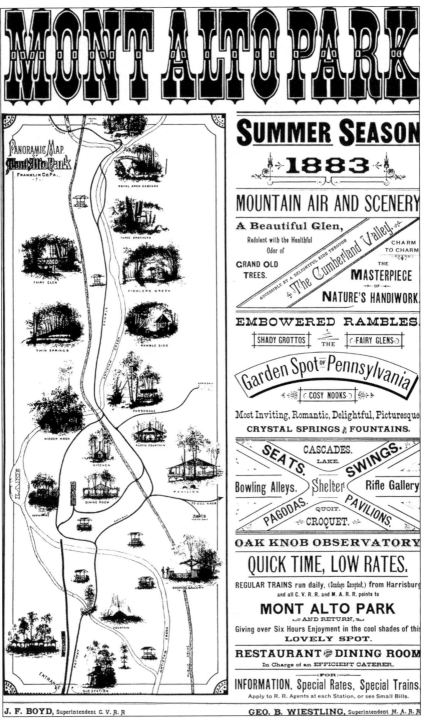

This reproduction of an 1883 poster touts the virtues of Mont Alto Park, which was older than the Pen Mar railway park by a few years. Using the Mont Alto Railroad branch, visitors came to the park from Harrisburg and other points along the Cumberland Valley Railroad line, and also from Maryland and West Virginia. (Courtesy of Becky Dietrich.)

The Rustic Bridge in Mont Alto Park was but one of many sites mentioned in 19th-century publicity flyers for the park. There were also the Fairy Glen, Fiddlers Green, Twin Spring, Hidden Nook, Rustic Fountain, dance pavilion, bowling alleys, quoit and croquet courts, a "commodious" dining room, a merry-go-round, and the "Pearl of the Park" spring. (Courtesy of Becky Dietrich.)

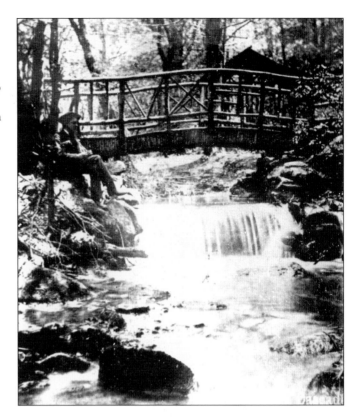

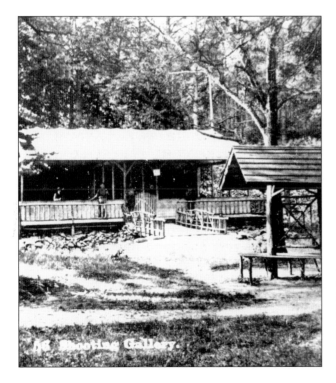

The shooting gallery, seen in the background, was one of many Mont Alto Park attractions that helped lure 19th-century urban dwellers to the area for a day of fun and relaxation. (Courtesy of Becky Dietrich.)

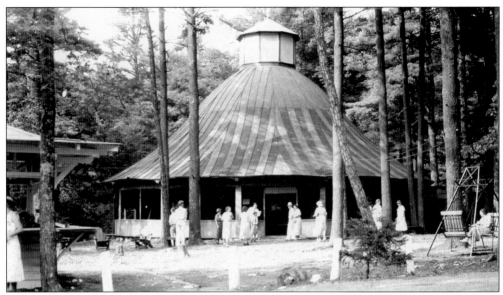

The Mont Alto Park pavilion, with its copper dome, still stands in Mont Alto State Park. Dances, band concerts, and family reunions were held regularly in this, the second dance pavilion. Visitors came by horse and buggy, cooling their drinks in the West Branch of the Little Antietam Creek. Some even brought fine linen and china to dine upon. (Courtesy of Becky Dietrich.)

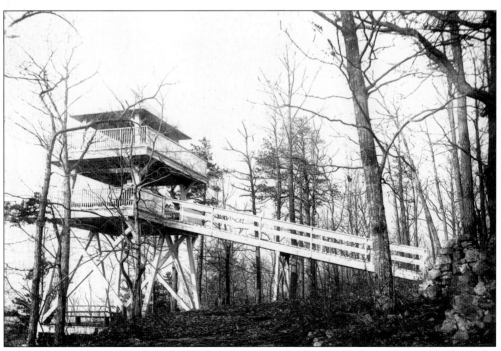

Mont Alto Park's popular Oak Knob Observatory was built *c.* 1875. It was located high on the mountainside over Mont Alto, more than 1,500 feet above sea level, 1,004 feet above Chambersburg, and 640 feet above the park entrance. (Courtesy of Becky Dietrich.)

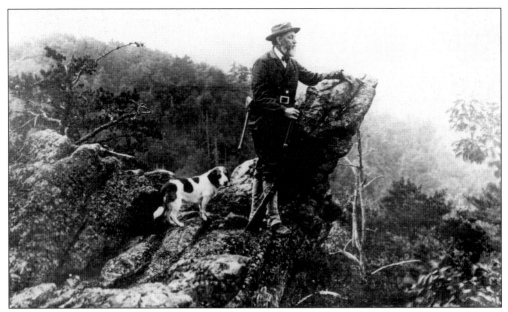

Dr. Joseph T. Rothrock was appointed Pennsylvania's first forestry commissioner and established the forest academy at Mont Alto in 1903. The Mont Alto Iron Company and a tract of more than 20,000 acres were sold to the state of Pennsylvania for a forestry reservation. (Courtesy of Becky Dietrich.)

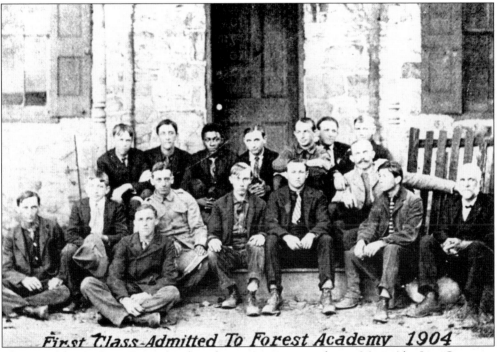

The Pennsylvania State Forest Academy began operations on former Mont Alto Iron Company land in 1903. This photograph is of the Class of 1904, the first admitted to the academy. In 1959, the campus was annexed by the borough of Mont Alto and became the Mont Alto campus of Pennsylvania State University. (Courtesy of Becky Dietrich.)

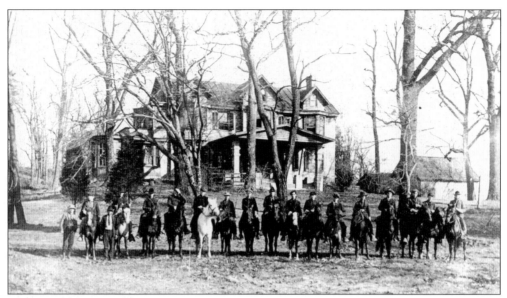

Forest Academy students pause on horseback in front of Wiestling Hall, which still stands on the Pennsylvania State University Mont Alto campus. Col. George B. Wiestling bought the Mont Alto Iron Company from the founding Hughes family in 1864. Wiestling modified the original log structure built in 1807 into the rambling Gothic Revival house in this photograph. Wiestling lived in the house until his death in 1891. (Courtesy of Becky Dietrich.)

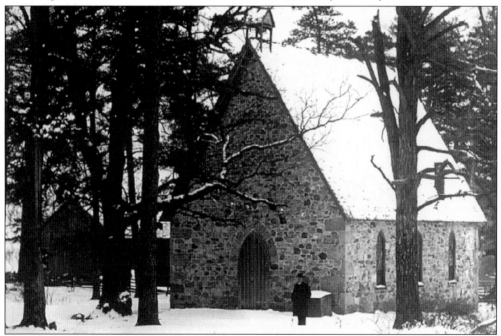

Emmanuel Chapel was built of native stone in 1854 by Mayor J. Holker Hughes of Mont Alto, who owned the Mont Alto Iron Company. It was the first Episcopal church west of the Blue Ridge Mountains in Pennsylvania. Legend has it that John Brown (alias Isaac Smith) worshiped here and taught Sunday school prior to the Harper's Ferry raid. The chapel still stands on the Penn State Mont Alto campus. (Courtesy of Becky Dietrich.)

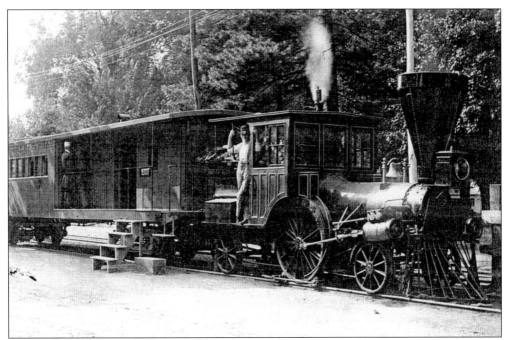

This small Pioneer locomotive, built in Boston in 1851, was used to haul loads on the Mont Alto Railroad line. It was known affectionately as the "Jenny Lind" and the "Toonerville." The railroad carried iron from the Mont Alto furnace, brought visitors to Mont Alto Park, and connected Waynesboro to the Cumberland Valley Railroad. (Courtesy of Becky Dietrich.)

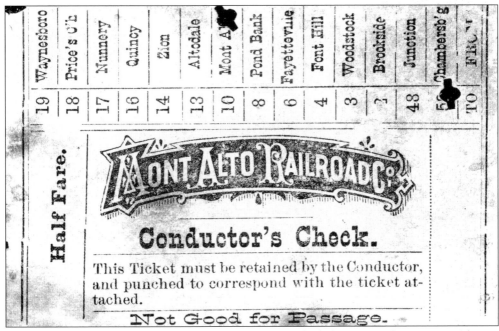

This Mont Alto Railroad conductor's check is punched for a trip from Mont Alto to Chambersburg. The first railroad conductor was Michael Kroner, and the train's station was called Alto Dale. (Courtesy of Becky Dietrich.)

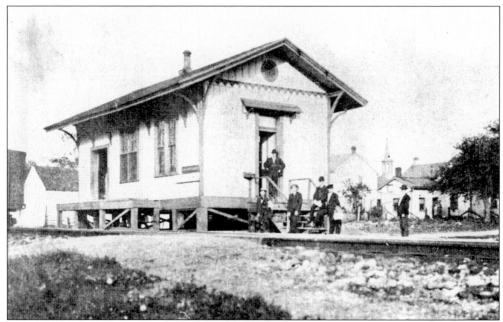

Mont Alto Railroad's freight station, built in 1872, was once located at the Mont Alto Iron works, where the Penn State campus is now located. It was moved years ago by rail to its present site off Penn Street, where it has served as a scout and teen center and a voting place. (Courtesy of Becky Dietrich.)

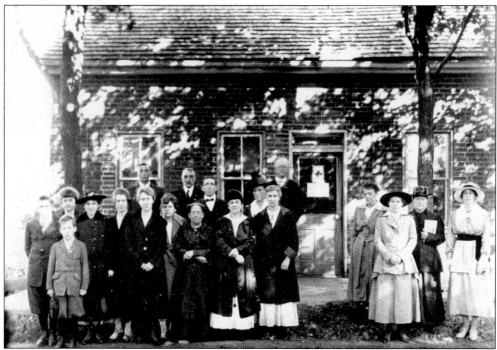

A Sunday school class poses in front of what is believed to be Mont Alto's original Evangelical United Brethren Church, which was built in 1851. The building stood on Water Street (now Penn Street). (Courtesy of Becky Dietrich.)

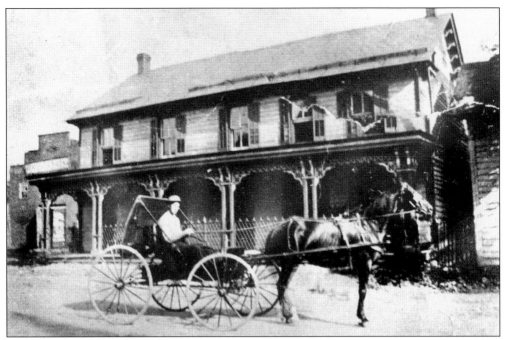

Shank's Hotel in Mont Alto was built in 1851. At one time there were three hotels in Mont Alto: Shank's, Clyde's, and the Union Hotel. The man in the buggy in this vintage photograph is Bob Small. (Courtesy of Becky Dietrich.)

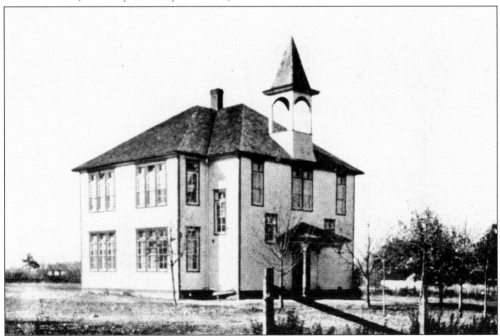

The Mont Alto public school building served the borough from 1897 to 1956, when a new school was built after operations were consolidated with Waynesboro. The school built in 1957 was shut down as part of a district consolidation, and the closest elementary school now is Mowrey, in Quincy Township. (Courtesy of Becky Dietrich.)

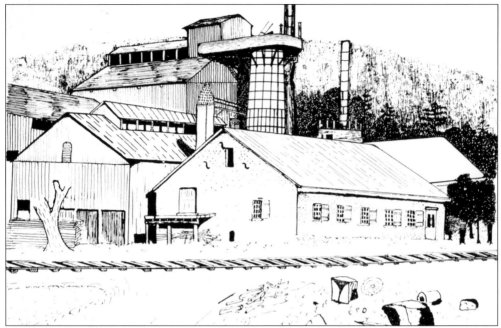

Founded in 1807 by Daniel, Samuel, and Holker Hughes, the Mont Alto Iron Company operated until 1892. Its operations expanded under Col. George Wiestling after 1864, and at its peak, the company employed more than 500 men. It took an acre of hardwood forest to run the furnace for one day, and competition from larger and more efficient coke furnaces sealed its doom. (Courtesy of Becky Dietrich.)

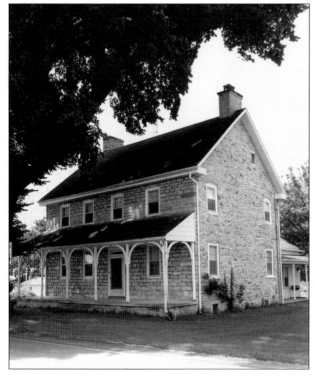

Knepper Station on Anthony Highway dates back to the 1790s. It was built by Abraham Knepper, who purchased 400 acres in 1782. Local tradition says that during the construction, loopholes were incorporated in the walls to protect workers from Delaware raiding parties. The loopholes are still visible on the inside of the house. (Courtesy of the Waynesboro Historical Society.)

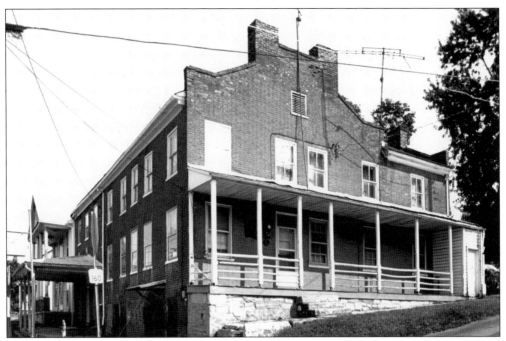

Recently damaged by fire, the Anderson Hotel on the square in Quincy Village was likely built by George Anderson in the 1850s. Local legend has it that Anderson, owner and manager of the hotel, poisoned Confederate troops who stopped to get a drink on their way to Gettysburg. Anderson is said to have later accidentally drunk from the unlabeled poisoned bottle and died on July 7, 1863. (Courtesy of the Waynesboro Historical Society.)

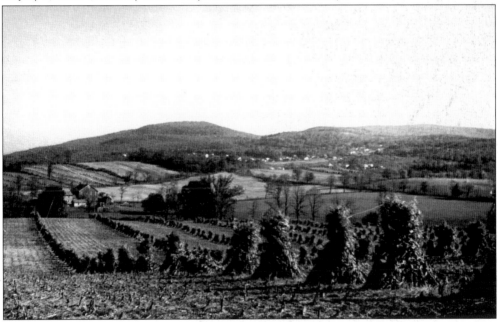

The rolling countryside surrounding Waynesboro has long been known for its scenic beauty, especially during the spring and at fall harvest time. This fall landscape by photographer Sylvester Snyder is titled *Mentzer Gap Country*. (Courtesy of Sylvester Snyder.)

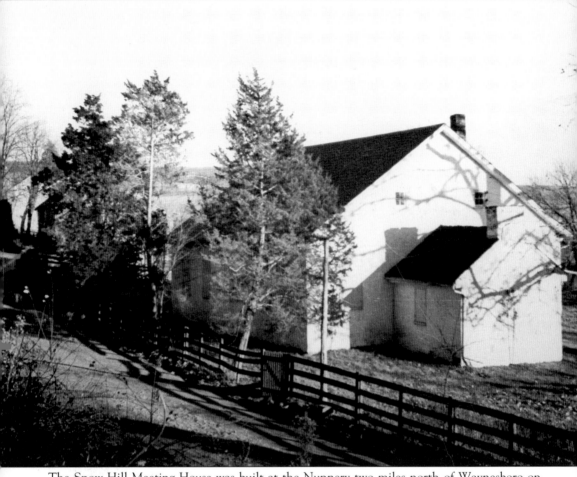

The Snow Hill Meeting House was built at the Nunnery two miles north of Waynesboro on Route 997 in 1929 by the Seventh Day Baptist Monastical Society, successor to the larger and more famous Ephrata Cloister. The Snow Hill Society of the German Seventh Day Baptists held weekly Saturday morning services in the meetinghouse into the 1980s. (Courtesy of Sylvester Snyder.)

Eight

Blue Ridge Summit and Pen Mar

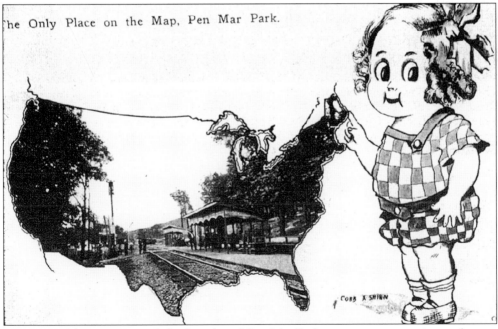

Promotional literature touted the benefits of Pen Mar Park as a summer vacation and resort area. In the park's early days, Blue Ridge Summit, 69 miles from Baltimore, had 16 hotels and cottages with rates from $1.50 to $2 per day, or $6 to $15 per week. Train fare from Baltimore was $2.07 to Blue Ridge Summit and $2.13 to Pen Mar. (Courtesy of Becky Dietrich.)

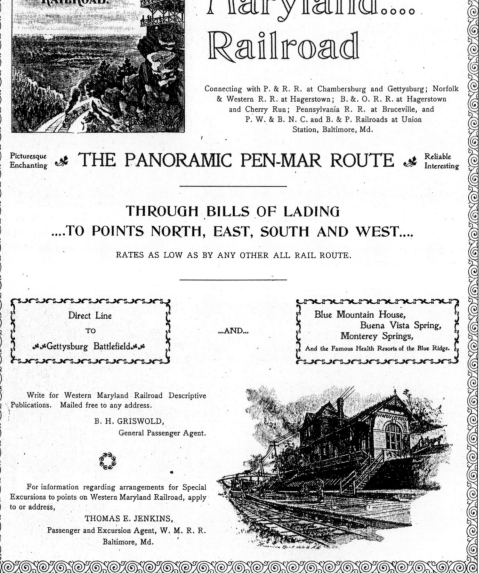

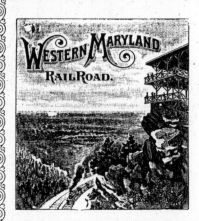

STEEL RAILS
MODERN EQUIPMENT

Western Maryland.... Railroad

Connecting with P. & R. R. at Chambersburg and Gettysburg; Norfolk
& Western R. R. at Hagerstown; B. &. O. R. R. at Hagerstown
and Cherry Run; Pennsylvania R. R. at Bruceville, and
P. W. & B. N. C. and B. & P. Railroads at Union
Station, Baltimore, Md.

Picturesque Enchanting ❧ **THE PANORAMIC PEN-MAR ROUTE** ❧ Reliable Interesting

THROUGH BILLS OF LADING
....TO POINTS NORTH, EAST, SOUTH AND WEST....

RATES AS LOW AS BY ANY OTHER ALL RAIL ROUTE.

Direct Line
TO
❧❧Gettysburg Battlefield❧❧

...AND...

Blue Mountain House,
Buena Vista Spring,
Monterey Springs,
And the Famous Health Resorts of the Blue Ridge.

Write for Western Maryland Railroad Descriptive
Publications. Mailed free to any address.

B. H. GRISWOLD,
General Passenger Agent.

For information regarding arrangements for Special
Excursions to points on Western Maryland Railroad, apply
to or address,

THOMAS E. JENKINS,
Passenger and Excursion Agent, W. M. R. R.
Baltimore, Md.

In the latter part of the 19th century, Western Maryland Railroad president John M. Hood figured a mountain resort area within easy reach of Baltimore and Washington would increase company revenues. With railroad help, the resorts of Blue Ridge Summit, Monterey, Pen Mar, and Blue Mountain House thrived. Hood also purchased the site of the future Pen Mar Park in 1871. (Courtesy of the Robert Ringer family.)

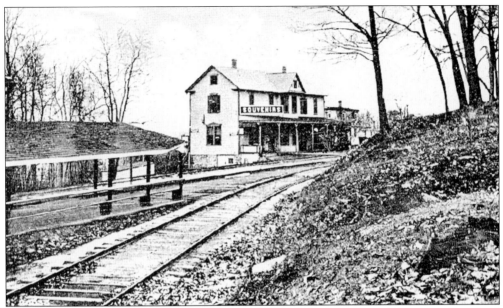

This postcard shows the station platform at Pen Mar, with the Pen Mar post office (and souvenir stand) in the background. Round-trip excursion fare from Baltimore to Pen Mar was as low as $1. Trains arrived before noon, and the last departure left at around 8:30 p.m. (Courtesy of Becky Dietrich.)

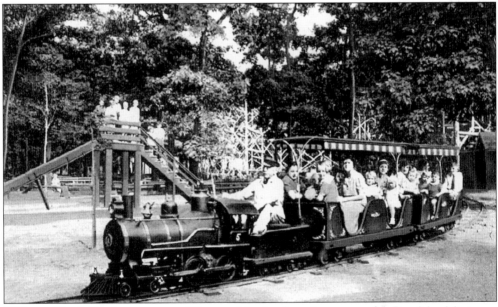

William "Pop" Fleigh, a veteran Western Maryland engineer, ran the Pen Mar Miniature Railway at Pen Mar Park. The ride, which first ran in 1904, was so popular that Fleigh got leave from the railroad to run it in the summer. By the 1920s, the railway had as many as 2,000 riders on Sundays. It was the last amusement attraction running when the park closed in 1942. (Courtesy of Becky Dietrich.)

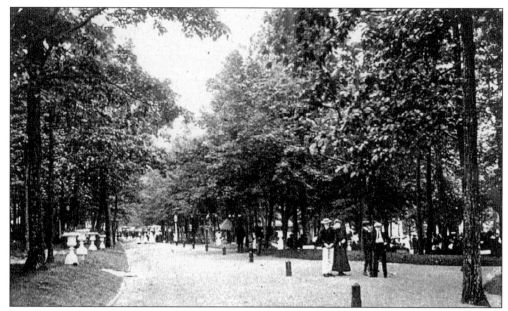

Pen Mar Park's shady promenade provided an ideal place for a Sunday stroll. In its heyday, the park attracted as many as 20,000 picnickers on a Sunday. Some people ate at the 450-seat dining hall, where full-course dinners were 50¢ and offered a choice of three meats and six vegetables, ice cream, and coffee served family style. (Courtesy of Becky Dietrich.)

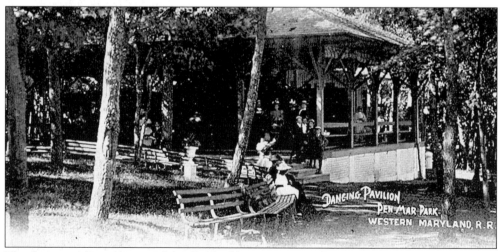

The dance pavilion was one of the first buildings constructed in Pen Mar Park, which opened on August 31, 1877. People often dashed under the pavilion's overhang to escape rain, and it provided space to listen to visiting orchestras and watch the dancers. Benches, both inside and out, offered a spot for pleasant conversation. (Courtesy of Becky Dietrich.)

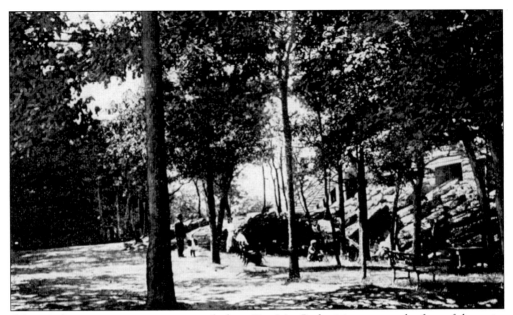

After a ride up a narrow mountain road, these Pen Mar Park visitors are at the foot of the stairs to the High Rock Observatory. In recent years, the road has been used by hang-gliding enthusiasts to reach a takeoff ramp atop High Rock. (Courtesy of Becky Dietrich.)

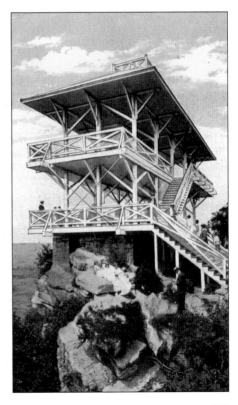

Horse-drawn hacks and large surreys took sightseers about a mile from Pen Mar Park to High Rock observatory in the late 1870s, when the Western Maryland Railroad cut a new road following the side of the mountain to the popular wooden observatory. The railroad brought visitors to the park from Washington and Baltimore for $1. (Courtesy of the Waynesboro Historical Society.)

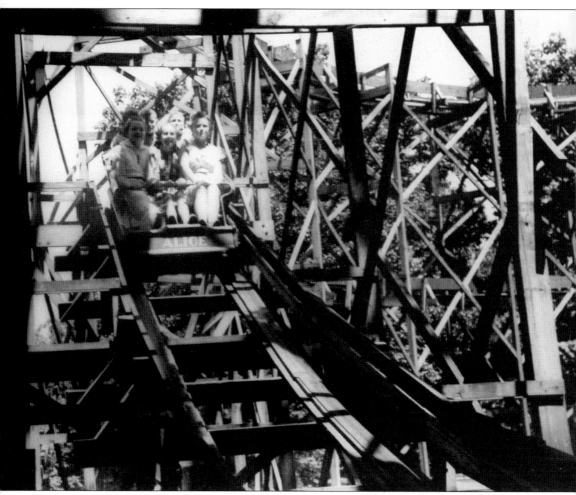

Passengers in the Alice car of the Pen Mar Park roller coaster enjoy a dip in 1938. The ride, built in 1909, was one of many attractions at Pen Mar, a popular railroad excursion park that entertained generations of visitors from 1877 until 1942. (Courtesy of Sylvester Snyder.)

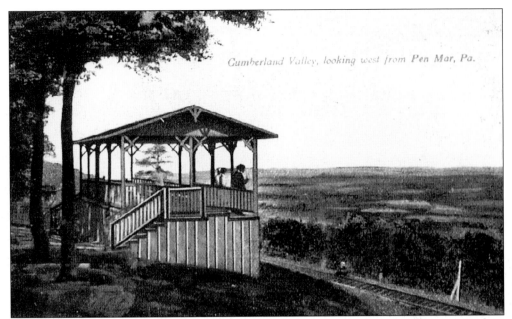

This scenic overlook, which provided a panoramic view of the Cumberland Valley to the west, was a popular spot for Pen Mar Park visitors. At the upper end of the park, horse-drawn vehicles waited to take park guests to High Rock, Mount Quirauk, or Ragged Edge for more scenic views. (Courtesy of Becky Dietrich.)

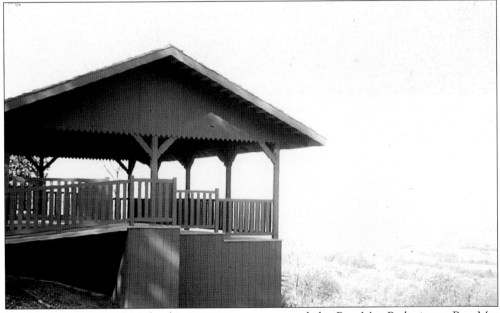

Washington County, Maryland, commissioners reopened the Pen Mar Park site as Pen Mar County Park in May 1977. Although the new park could not match the amusement grandeur of the old park, a scenic lookout pavilion representing the old one was installed. The park also has a dance pavilion once again, which attracts big crowds to weekend concerts. (Courtesy of Becky Dietrich.)

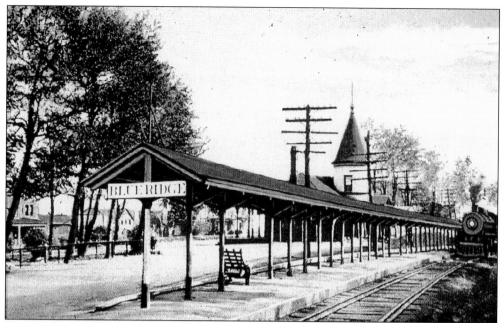

The Blue Ridge Summit train station was built in 1891 as part of the Western Maryland Railroad service from Baltimore to Hagerstown. It was one of several stations serving resort areas near Pen Mar Park. Blue Ridge Summit was once the vacation home of 16 foreign embassies. The Queen Anne–style station at Monterey Avenue now serves as the Blue Ridge Summit Free Library. (Courtesy of Becky Dietrich.)

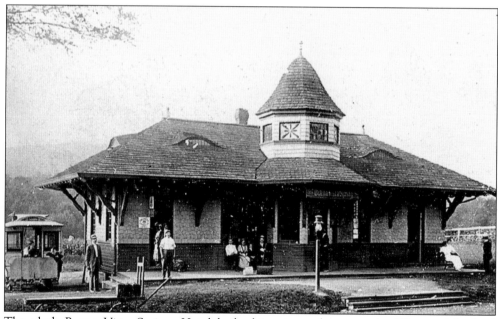

The plush Buena Vista Springs Hotel built this private depot on the Western Maryland Railroad line at Cascade. In April 1891, a telephone line between the hotel and Buena Vista Station was completed. The trolley on the left, pulled by two horses, took guests up a steep road 2 1/2 miles to the hotel. The trolley tracks were torn up in 1922. (Courtesy of Becky Dietrich.)

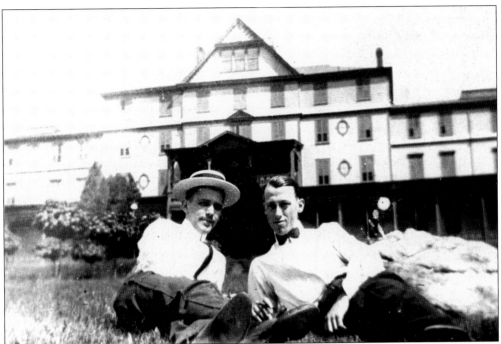

Harry Spoonhour, left, and John H.C. Dick of Waynesboro relax in front of the Blue Mountain House at Pen Mar in 1911. It would be one of the last seasons to enjoy the rambling resort hotel, which burned to the ground in 1913. (Courtesy of the Waynesboro Historical Society.)

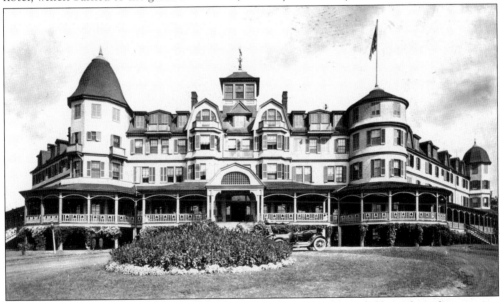

The lavish Buena Vista Springs Hotel, built in 1890, was one of several luxury hostelries serving the mountainous resort area above Waynesboro in the late 19th and early 20th centuries. Guests included members of Pres. Woodrow Wilson's family, Secretary of the Treasury McAdoo, Admiral Dewey, Pres. Manuel Quezon of the Philippines, various U.S. ambassadors, and actress Joan Crawford. The hotel was destroyed by fire in 1967. (Courtesy of the Waynesboro Historical Society.)

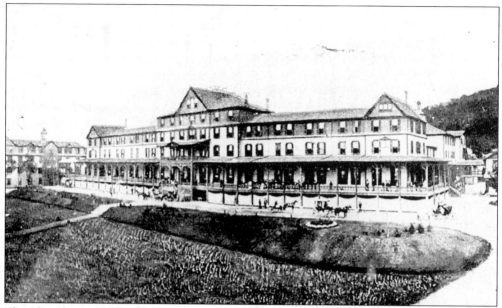

The Blue Mountain House, one of the most famous Blue Ridge Mountain resorts, was built in 76 working days in 1883 at a cost of $225,000. A broad porch formed a 700-foot promenade around the building, which could accommodate 500 guests. Its site was about a mile below Pen Mar and 600 feet above the Western Maryland tracks. Initial room rates were $3 to $5 a day. (Courtesy of Becky Dietrich.)

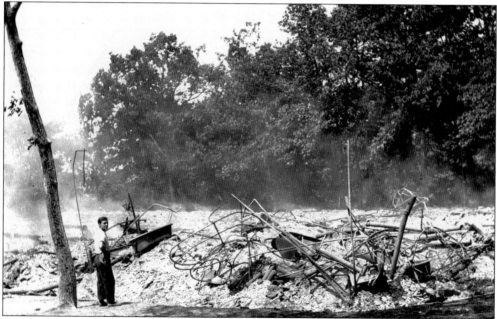

On August 5, 1913, a guest at the Blue Mountain House noticed smoke coming from under the porch. The alarm was spread, and 250 guests scurried from the building. Within three hours, the hotel that had once housed Pres. Woodrow Wilson and Grover Cleveland was in ruins. The fire started in a porter's room, where it was believed the wind blew a curtain into a burning gas jet flame. (Courtesy of the Robert Ringer family.)

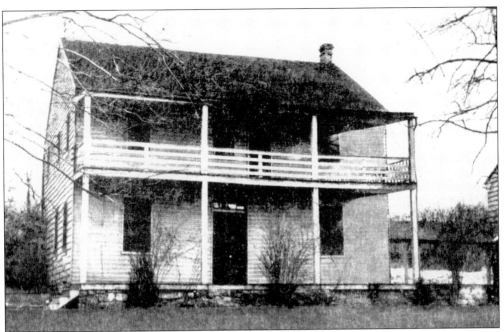

Square Cottage was the birthplace of Wallis Warfield Simpson, duchess of Windsor. It was located on the grounds of the former Monterey Inn at Old Route 16 and Monterey Lane. Wallis Warfield was born June 19, 1896. Her mother, Alys Warfield, was attended by Dr. Lewis Allen, who took a train from Baltimore, where the Warfields resided, to Blue Ridge Summit. Square Cottage was razed in 1942. (Courtesy of Becky Dietrich.)

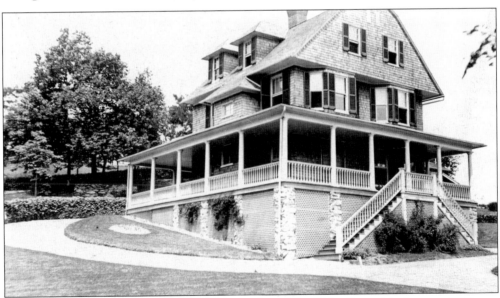

Monterey Circle in Charmian (now incorporated into Blue Ridge Summit), shown c. 1909, was previously known as Rocky Spring Park. A new Monterey Inn was opened on the circle in 1958 by a retired navy reserve commander for the exclusive use of military people. The inn had seven bedrooms and a huge dining room catered by "Strig" Potter of Greencastle. (Courtesy of the Waynesboro Historical Society.)

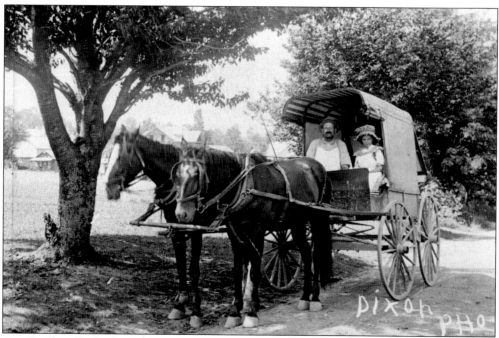

Aquilla Fox, who had a meat shop on his farm, is shown delivering meat in Blue Ridge Summit *c.* 1909 with his daughter, Emma. Horses Prince and Pete are pulling the wagon. (Courtesy of Becky Dietrich.)

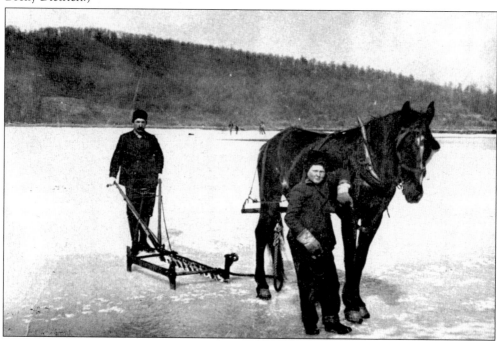

Joseph J. Fox leads Pete, who is pulling a marker plow, while Alfred Nichols works the plow to score and mark ice on Lake Royer for the Buena Vista Ice Company *c.* 1911. The ice was supplied to the Pen Mar and Waynesboro regions. Lake Royer was a popular boating and ice-skating spot during the resort era. (Courtesy of Becky Dietrich.)

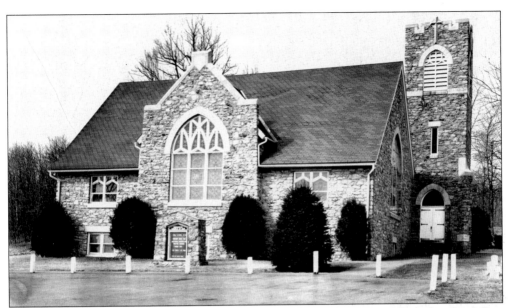

Germantown Bethel Church of God stands atop South Mountain near Cascade, above Fort Ritchie. Cascade was known as "Germantown" until World War I, and the name "Cascade" comes from the great falls on Falls Creek between Fort Ritchie and Buena Vista. The church was built by the Browns, a family of stonemasons. Their ancestor, William Browne, came to the country in 1634 as a manservant and shoemaker. (Courtesy of the Robert Ringer family.)

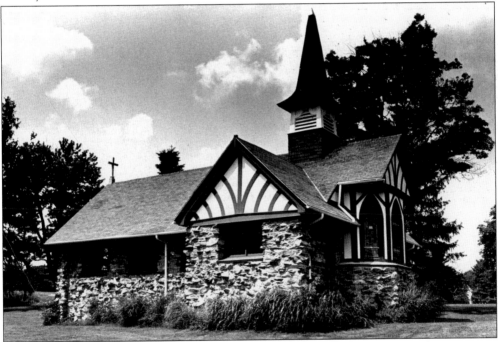

Robert E. Rennert Memorial Chapel, which stands near the site of the former Buena Vista Springs Hotel, was given by Mrs. Rennert in memory of her husband, who died in 1898. The chapel was dedicated on July 18, 1900. A Baltimore hotelier, Rennert was involved in establishing the Buena Vista in 1891. (Courtesy of Sid Miller, the *Record Herald*.)

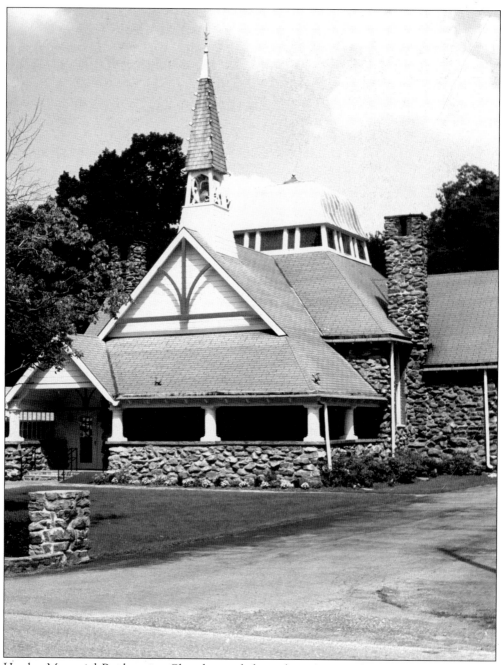

Hawley Memorial Presbyterian Church was dedicated on August 10, 1889, as a memorial to Martin Hawley, an architect from Baltimore. The chapel, located along Charmian Road at Monterey, is said to be a replica of a church in Czechoslovakia. (Courtesy of the Waynesboro Historical Society.)